"STOP ASKING FOR PERMISSION & GIVE NOTICE!"

A GUIDE TO LIVING UNAPOLOGETICALLY

Charron Monaye

Foreword by Lucinda Cross

Pen Legacy

"Stop Asking for Permission & Give Notice!", Copyright © 2016 by Charron Monaye. All rights reserved. Printed in the United States of America. No part of this publication may be distributed, reproduced or transmitted in any form, without the permission of the publisher except in the case of brief quotations embodied and cited in critical articles or reviews, etc.

First Edition

Designed By Junnita Jackson
Front Photo by: John Lampkins of Shooterz Photos
Back Photos by: Brenda Lee
Photography and Make-Up Artist: Brenda Lee
Edited by: Renise Welbon of CheckDoubleCheck

Library of Congress Cataloging – in- Publication Data has been applied for.

DEDICATION:

This book is dedicated to my children, Christopher and Craig. Finally, Mommy got it!! Our journey has not been the easiest, but we have, at last, found our way to easier days, sunnier mornings, and the nights are no longer, as long as they used to be. You have witnessed me at my weakest, and have protected me through my trials, and because of your love, smiles, and support, I am stronger than ever. You are the inspiration and motivation behind the happiness that I bear within ME! I am so proud of the young men you are becoming and everyday #TeamHopson continues to get better… I AM because YOU are THERE.

I think it's time for a Vacation! We deserve it!!!

Love you both…
Mommy

Permission: Defined

PERMISSION

~ noun

- The right or ability to do something that is given by someone who has the power to decide if it will be allowed or permitted
- An official document giving authorization.
- Consent

Notice: Defined

NOTICE

~ noun

- Attention that people give to someone or something
- A written or printed announcement
- notification or warning of something, especially to allow preparations to be made.

CONTENTS

Foreword By Lucinda Cross

Introduction

Part 1 — 1

There is Power in Your Notice! — 2

Two Weeks Notice Lose To Win — 26

Personal Ownership — 39

The 3 A's ~ Acknowledge, Acceptance, Attainment — 49

Acknowledge — 50

Acceptance — 56

Attainment — 60

To Keep It or Return It — 75

What is your Intention? — 84

Welcome to the New Life — 88

Part 2

30 Days of Self-Transformation Daily Activities — 94

FOREWORD
BY LUCINDA CROSS

As a Master Coach, I have had the pleasure of coaching thousands from procrastination and one common thread that they all shared was seeking validation for their God given purpose. That is why, when Charron Monaye asked me to write the foreword I said "Yes" immediately. This is a book; I wish I had when I left corporate America in 2006. Lack of direction, instruction and seeking permission to follow my dreams was what held me back from pursuing many opportunities in my journey of entrepreneurship.

In "STOP Asking for Permission & Give Notice", bestselling author Charron Monaye will lead you, step-by-step, to a greater understanding of your own past, your motivations, and your desires. Once you have completed this book and have done self-examination, you will be able to move beyond your seeking validation and into living a life of fire, fun and freedom. Our lifestyle is designed and crafted based on the way we project and perceive things. Are you allowing your limiting beliefs to place a blockage on manifesting your vision? Many people have a millionaire vision, a dollar and a dream mindset and poor language. In order for me to enjoy the lifestyle that I am living now, I had to change the words I used, the thoughts I had and the conversations I engaged in. Basically I had to give myself permission to succeed.

Charron Monaye brilliantly illustrates this importance of owning your life in the keys and strategies that are shared and the advice she provides. I can tell you without reservation or question that when it comes to giving yourself permission, she is the trusted advisor and industry leader in this subject matter. I know this because I have enjoyed the opportunity of observing her extraordinary success strategies and principles she teaches that have proven effective. STOP Asking for Permission & Give Notice is intended to be applied in a synergistic way. Fully engage yourself in the advice given. Write down ways that you can include some of the advice to your personal life. I challenge you to apply just one of these strategies, and I look forward to hearing your testimony.

Life is worth living, so start living today,

Lucinda Cross
Founder of Activate WorldWide Inc.
Best Selling Author, Award Winning Speaker, TV Personality and America's Favorite Vision Board Queen.
www.lucindacross.com

PART 1

ARE YOU READY TO DO THE WORK???

THERE IS POWER IN YOUR NOTICE!

There is a big difference between you asking for permission to live in your own purpose, and you dictating that YOU are going to live in YOUR purpose. Far too often, we wait for someone or something to validate our greater purpose in life. We dream of something better, only to watch our futures bypass us in our minds. We are mired in our mindsets, refusing to achieve anything because we feel that we require some sort of "permission slip" from society, to become who we have always desired to be, to realize the lives that we have always visualized. Have you ever dreamed of your own successes? Have they ever seemed so real to you that you could touch the rewards within your own imagination? Have you ever watched your visions play out in your mind and felt like it was even possibly obtainable? Now, after these dreams and visions have slowly faded away, what steps or actions did you take in order to progress towards making those dreams a reality? We all sit and mentally see our future and who we feel we are destined to be, but very few of us know how, or when, to make the moves necessary to give the required notice, that will bring us from the dream into the reality!

When you give notice to someone, you remove from them the power of their opinion, suggestion, or any thought they may have that will be used to deter you from your required action. Giving notice, as it says in the definition above, allows those around you to prepare themselves for what it is that you are declaring that you WILL do! When you give notice to others as to WHO you are, WHAT you are intending to accomplish, WHEN the actions will transpire, HOW everything will be played out, and WHY it is all necessary, ultimately shows not only that you are independent, but that you understand your own calling and believe in that calling enough to move forward towards it in faith. Some would say that the idea of giving notice rather than asking for permission to do something, especially within your own life, is "cocky". In my opinion, waiting for someone to grant you permission to be your authentic self, is completely debasing to self. Everyone who is born is given a calling on their life, a purpose to fulfill, a passion to enjoy, and a love to share with others. They are given these attributes by God, or through their D.N.A., or both, to help them have a life that will be rewarding and beneficial to themselves, and to those who enjoy their company. They were not given the resources to live an abundant life, only to later have to ask permission to use those resources. For example, people were not given the gift of a voice to sing, only to have to ask others for permission to use that gift of song, and for how long! No! They were given that voice to share, and the ability to tell others when and where they would be sharing their gift on any given night.

We have to stop allowing people the ability to decide the fate of our gifts, resources, and attributes that are inherent with the life we are given. If it was not meant for us to have these gifts and resources, then I am certain that we would not have been blessed with any of them. I am here to coach, inspire, and motivate you to start notifying people of what you want and who you are, while confirming it all with actionable measures that are satisfying to you. Living life can be risky and scary. Taking chances can be uncomfortable and challenging. However, making the plan to try, and working the plan to actual BE authentic to who you are, is the best thing you could ever do for yourself. Often, I have conversations with people who have yet to find fulfillment in their lives, who have fewer memories or successes attributed to themselves because they were so involved in taking care of, and catering to others. When asked why they made the decision to put themselves last, some replied, *"**Because I am waiting for permission to be first**"*. Others stated *"**I am waiting for the time to get back to me**"*. A few said, *"**I'm waiting for someone to come along and give me the tools to make it in this competitive society**"*. After hearing those answers, my questions then to these people were, "Who are you waiting for, and what tools can't you get on your own?" If this is a competitive society, then why do you expect someone who is IN the race to help you enter the race, or give you anything that will allow you the opportunity to bypass him or her in the race? Granted, there are those few who might be willing to share their journey and resources with you. There are the few who may be willing to mentor or coach you to your destiny, while striving for their own. Speaking from experience, those rare folks are so few and far between, that you will be more likely to run into someone praying for your downfall, instead of trying to help you rise to meet your potential.

"Stop Asking for Permission & Give Notice!" is a book designed to give yourself your "*hall pass*" to live your life in a manner that is authentic to you, without having to apologize for your personal decisions. You will be given the necessary tools to start giving notice to the world as to the Who, What, When, How, and Why you are irrepressible! You will be unapologetic when it comes to your choices, and unbothered when it comes to your choice of lifestyle. You will learn how to be resilient when it comes to defeat, and enlightened when it comes to letting go. In order to live life according to your own purpose, you have to first acknowledge and accept who you are. When you can define who you are, incorporating the remaining puzzle pieces into the framework of your life will be much more attainable. Now before you say, "Charron said I can go out and do me", let me make sure you are clear on what you are announcing. Do you have a dream you wish to fulfill? Are you living your life vicariously through someone else because you do not have enough faith within yourself to accomplish the successes on your own? Are you waiting for the proverbial opportunity to knock on your door? Are you anticipating that someone will deliver to your doorstep the success that you need to make you the next best thing in America? Are you hoping for a "YES" from someone to validate that your goals can be achieved? Living life is not about being reckless or negative in order to get what you deem to be necessary, but about recognizing and setting forth on the journey that aligns with your calling and purpose! You can only expect to receive what you make known that you want, and this book will help you do just that.

We will leave the concept of seeking validation and asking for permission right here, because we no longer need to do any of that. There are enough resources, tools, life coaches and Google websites that we can use to create our own YES when the world tells us NO, or attempts to force us into a position of DELAY and WAIT! Effective IMMEDIATELY, we will not ask the world for anything, but instead TELL the world everything, announcing our arrival...hence...GIVING OUR NOTICE!!!

Before we move forward, please answer the following coaching questions so that you can identify the issues that are delaying you, while preparing your mindset on how to move forward.

What have you been asking permission to do?
_____
_____
_____
_____

What is the most important personal characteristic within yourself that that makes you believe you are worthy?
_____
_____
_____
_____

To understand your journey, are you able to identify at least one thing you want to achieve in your life?

_____
_____
_____
_____

To accept your failures as lessons, consider the things you have not been successful with and why. Now, which one of those things has taught you the greatest lesson, and describe that lesson in detail?

_____
_____
_____
_____

TWO-WEEKS NOTICE

I can remember the first time I heard Lisa Nicols say, *"Stop asking the worlds permission to get you. Give the world notice that you are coming!"* Ms. Nicols, who is a motivational speaker, author, and the C.E.O of Motivating the Masses, was transforming my mindset to help me accept who I am, flaws and all. She made me stop keeping score on everything I got wrong in life, and forced me to start investing my energy and time into everything I actually got right. She tutored me on how to learn from the things with which I was struggling. After hearing her speak and then reading her books, I realized that I needed to fall madly in love with ME! *The Real ME!* In addition to Lisa Nichols, I experienced additional transformation, as a result, of my conversations with Vaughn McNeill, author and co-worker, who confirmed for me that, "**my choices where mine and people had to respect them**". Now I need you to STOP…and just think about that for a minute… Through daily conversations and hardcore truths and judgment about me, I realized that my voice and my life were not always mine. I felt that I was living on time that was on loan to me…NOT my own time. It was time spent only to assist others, to wait for others, or to look for others to agree with my choices. I had lived most of my life up until that point doing what was right for others, but what was wrong for me. I often allowed people to talk me out of my desires simply because I let them make me believe that the idea seemed dumb, lacked financial feasibility, or was unrealistic to them, so it should then seem unattainable to me. Now I will admit, being a single mother and investing my life and money into my dream of being an acclaimed writer, did not guarantee rewards, but NOT doing what I loved was tantamount to my committing emotional suicide. I couldn't win! However, coming to the understanding that

I am a mother first and a writer second, I often jeopardized my dream of writing many times, in the interest of living a life more accepted as "normal" to those around me. I tried to stop writing my poetry, I tried reducing myself to only talking through my feelings as a "normal" person is expected to do…only to start having anxiety attacks and horrible mood swings.

I can remember being so full of emotional distress and conversations that I felt incapable of verbalizing that I would come home and take out all my frustrations on my sons. I would explode for no reason at all. They would be playing with their toys, like boys do, and anything from the noise they were making to the sound of their voices would annoy me. With any small provocation, I would find myself yelling. I was out of control! My epiphany came when my oldest son apologized to me for being loud. I realized that they are kids, doing exactly what kids SHOULD be doing, and it was me who was in the wrong! In what world should my son feel he should be apologizing for being a kid and playing as kids should? It was in that moment, that I knew that the "normal" that was acceptable for others, was not for me. I am naturally an introverted person, not one who easily communicates verbally. I am capable of talking about my feelings, but I am more comfortable and secure in the expression of my emotions if I am able to write them. With this realization, I gave myself permission to resume my writing. I picked up my pen, and I opened up my book, and almost immediately, the house went back to being quiet (because I stopped yelling unnecessarily), and there was a return to our typical peaceful routine. After that experience, and because of that lesson, I learned that writing IS my "normal", and that even if I am not pursuing this as a career to bring fame and fortune, I MUST write daily.

Now, I must ask, how many of you are living your life according to someone else's definition of normal, and attempting to force yourself into their defined mold? Are you giving yourself permission to insist that others respect your choices in life, whether they agree with them or not? We did not enter into this Life with an instruction manual. We have not been given instructions on how to navigate childhood, or becoming a smashingly successful adult.

Everyday we live life, we are either learning as we go, or missing the mark that might lead us to what will make us greater. However, there are resources and networks that are available to each one of us, resources and networks which are willing and ready to help us to see where we want to be, and what we need to do to get there. This realization was so fundamental for me because I knew I was supposed to be something greater than what I already was, but I had no idea how to get there. I had no realistic plan, nor did I have a financially feasible resource to execute a plan. And more importantly, I still did not have enough confidence in myself to further invest! I still needed someone else's opinion to validate my dreams. So when Lisa Nicols said, *"Stop asking the worlds permission to get you. Give the world notice that you are coming!"*, her words resonated with me. I realized that I needed to apply this transformative decree to my own life. When I originally started giving notice, the first thing I did was acknowledge and eliminate all unnecessary baggage, dead weight, and negative influences from my life. I looked at my personal contacts (friends and family), social media (followers and friends), daily habits, and how I was treating myself (with love or without love). I cannot begin to tell you how much negativity was surrounding me, that I was not even aware was there. I felt the need to give myself a "toxicity cleansing" day. In other words, I deleted, threw away, ended, and closed access to many people in my life, on my timelines, and in my cell phone. I re-evaluated my responses to ME and how I was treating myself, as well as how I was allowing others to treat me, and I vowed to insist on receiving the respect and love I was due, especially from myself. Have you ever heard the saying "You are the company that you keep"? You cannot aspire to be anything great, when people who are comfortable living in mediocrity surround you. You cannot expect to exceed the worlds limitations, if you surround yourself with people who have succumbed to the limits set forth for them, often by their own mindsets. Therefore, it is imperative to let go of anything that is stopping you from being who you want to be. Letting go can be the HARDEST thing to do, but you will APPRECIATE the liberation once you have accomplished it! During my "toxicity cleansing", I forced myself to let go of things, people, experiences, and fears that no longer had any purpose or position in my life. I could not keep the old stuff in my life because that "stuff" was the main reason that I was incapable of owning my life, and unable to make choices on my own and be confident in them once made. You can't move forward holding on to the ideas of yesterday. Eventually your past will cloud your judgment and bring your forward progression into your new journey to a grinding halt. A halt that will cause you to second-guess your choices, or even permit others to convince you to give up on what you have been fighting for, just because they are not able to grasp the greatness that is within you.

Let's Have an Open and Honest Conversation:

Have you ever remained in a relationship with someone longer than you should have? Can you calculate the price you paid for staying past your curfew? Was it worth the time, or did it cause you to resent the other person, or even yourself? I was in a relationship with a man whom I knew was using me, verbally abusing me, and taking advantage of my "giving" nature. I knew he wasn't good for me, but because he was comfortable and familiar to my life story, I allowed him to remain, and I gave him permission to mistreat me. Everything he did was normalized for me, but my intuition told me that once he attained the level he was seeking, he was going to leave anyway. I had every sign, feeling, and tangible proof that should have screamed to me that he was not the one, but still, I stayed. I carried his hurtful baggage and nurtured his past wounds thinking that I had what it took to show him a different future. However, my efforts, at times, were faced with yelling matches, blaming parties, and confrontational meetings. I found excuses and gave him a pass for everything I did not enjoy. I gave him so many second chances that it became impossible for me to distinguish the difference between his disrespect for me, and my lack of respect for myself…it was all so entangled, and impossible to unravel. I was numb. I became the hurt he inflicted, and allowed him to write a new chapter of my life, one that I could not recognize, but would make him the center of it. I knew this was not my story, but because I was comfortable in his world, and had adapted to his toxic behavior and started to mimic it, letting go was terrifying. I stop writing as much as I needed to, and started focusing on his journey. I began investing myself and my time solely to fixing his life because as a good woman, you are told to "hold your man down" because "if you don't, someone else will". Since I did not want to lose a man again (yes, I can admit it), I did what I needed to keep that man happy. However, keeping him happy, denied me the right to be myself, completely. My requesting permission was constantly met with arguments and refusals. So much so that I eventually gave up asking and just became content living in the confusion that I had allowed to be created for me. Sometimes, when it became too much, I would leave him or ask him to leave, only to return looking and hoping for the change he promised me. I, often times, blamed myself for our problems because in his eyes, everything that was wrong with us was my fault. Nevertheless, after 3 years, he eventually walked away from me, and stayed gone. It was in him walking away, that I finally found the strength to let go myself. Even though I knew he was going to leave, I realized that our relationship not only robbed me of years, it also taught me to choose and love myself first.

His heartless rejection gave me the strength to begin to work on elevating my self-esteem. No one should have the power to walk into your life and disrupt it to the point that you are no longer able to recognize who you are, where you are going, and where you should be. I found that I had to give myself a second chance by hitting the reset button on MYSELF! I had to be reintroduced to myself because who I knew myself to be, and who I had become, was not adding up in this life that I was living. Therefore, I took a time-out on life and rebuilt my persona, from the inside out. Redefined what I was willing to accept, reconfirmed the "WHY" of being ME, and why loving MYSELF was necessary, NOT occasionally optional! When you are true to yourself and know who you are, allowing a relationship like the one described in the previous pages would not happen. He was able to violate so many boundaries, and I permitted myself to lower my own standards to the degree that I had hit bottom and could go no lower than where I lay, crying to find solace from the pain of this unrecognizable life I was enduring.

That was how I knew that his leaving was God's plan for me. He saw that I was not strong enough to let go on my own, and through my actions of trying to let go he felt that, *enough was truly enough*. Of course, He knew best. After sitting down one day acknowledging my mistakes, accepting my role in maintaining the madness, and comprehending the lessons so I do not repeat, I was able to retreat, and begin to renew. I found access to the best version of me. I started discovering things about me that I was not aware existed. I did so by answering the following questions:

> *What was it about him that made you so comfortable that you allowed yourself to be denigrated by him? Who did he remind you of?*
>
> *Do you love yourself? Do you love yourself ENOUGH?*
>
> *Are you able to accept that situation as an experience that you need to learn a lesson from? Are you WILLING to identify the lesson and acknowledge the truths that the lesson will provide?*
>
> *Are you able to admit your faults and implement the lessons that can be learned from this situation?*

Are you able to FORGIVE yourself?

HOW will you begin the journey to move forward from this place in your life? WHAT will be your first step?

I shared that conversation with you because it had every "wrong" element of life in it. It also shows the start of my correcting those "wrongs". My relationship not only showed how difficult it is to release toxic things (or people), but also that you can not live YOUR life when someone else is in control of it. I could not be who I needed to be, because his negativity held me hostage in the belief that "I" was impossible, and I had adopted his beliefs as my law. However, even though I can go on and on about what we did, eventually I had to do some honest evaluation, and force myself to own my **Own Actions**, and lack of action as well. The first thing I realized that I should not have done was allow him to have power over my life. I permitted his word to be the law in my life, and I did not question his motives, or his intent. I did not fight for my dream. I gave up on myself. I refused to fight for either of them because I felt that his dreams were more important. I allowed him to treat me in a way that I knew deep inside, I did not deserve. I knew in my heart that I deserved so much better. However, this mistreatment afforded me the lesson that I needed which helped me to identify and set very specific boundaries that are in place for those who should enter my life from this point on, whether on an intimate level, a friendship level, or even a business level. There are now set expectations that will need to be met by anyone who wants to interact with me. Setting boundaries, limitations, and clear expectations in your life is so necessary. They help to eliminate sometimes-unforeseeable problems or baggage, before they grow into something you can't control. These same boundaries, limits, and expectations can also help to predict problems, and allow you the opportunity to make moves to avoid them before they become YOUR problems. Even though, this was a painful experience, it was one of the best things that could have happened. It made me own myself. It forced me to re-evaluate my own treatment of myself, and led me to the decision to change my perception and perspective. As a result, I change how I treated ME, and how I allowed others to treat me. ***People treat you, how you treat you!***

Today you will need to wade through every aspect of your world and see what you can get rid of, and what you need to say goodbye to. Take a minute and think about everything and everyone that is distracting you from your goals, your dreams, and from obtaining the life you desire. Then think about why these obstacles were there in the first place. Understanding why someone or something is in our lives is extremely important, especially when attempting to identify whether or not something needs to be disposed of, because we learn more about who we really are, from the people and things that we allow to have space in our lives. Sometimes we create our own burdens to carry. We link with dead weight because we ourselves are dead weight. I always tell people, "We attract who we are subconsciously". Meaning, we are more compelled to be around like-minded individuals because it's easier to relate to them, and nine times out of ten, we see ourselves when we are looking at them. It is imperative to understand that the energy that you attract, IS who you are. You will never be able to live the life you want, if you continue to harbor things that prove to be a detriment to your unhampered existence. Eventually you are going to have to choose between your dreams and what is comfortable. If my conversation thus far reminds you of you right now, I challenge you to write a "Two Weeks Notice", resigning yourself from that mindset and lifestyle. I had to learn that I am enough, you will have to learn the same. I had to realize that I am not perfect, you will have to accept the same. I had to recognize that in spite of my imperfections, I don't deserve anything in my life that will deter me from living. You will need to acknowledge the same in order for your life to begin to move to a place that you can live without permission from others. Living for me is something that is priceless and can't be compromised. Life is too short to have negativity deny you the freedom to own your existence. You were given life for a purpose, and it's time for you to own it, and live it unapologetically. Since I have taken the responsibility to live my life, I have less stress, I tolerate very little drama, and when I see it coming, I remove myself from its path, and most importantly, I love me to the fullest! I have expectations and standards that I hold myself, and those around me, too. I have restructured my life into one that I can now say that I am proud of. I am happy with me and I enjoy being with me simply because I decided to resign my position from the life that wasn't viable for me anymore. It was not fulfilling, and I knew I had so much more to offer if I took my assets elsewhere. Take a minute and visualize how your life is similar to the job you hold and work so hard at every day? Think about it:

> You wake up every day to make your way to the end of each day in your journey – **you wake up every day and make your way to your daily job....**
>
> You work hard to make your life what you want it to be – **you work hard to do well on your job to allow you to be comfortable while you are there....**
>
> Your failures are your lessons or teachable moments on what to do better – **your mistakes and disciplinary actions on your job teach you to do better and give you lessons to learn to improve in your day-to-day performance...**
>
> Your successes in life pay you forward to live in abundance – **your successes in your daily job pay you in salary increases and promotions...**
>
> There is always room to advance by networking – **there is always room to advance in your day to day job or field by networking...**

The similarities and comparisons are endless! Life can be a job, and a job can become a life! Everything in our lives are connected to another area of our lives, or be used to improve upon what we already have. You should always want to improve your life, in the same way you would want to improve your career, relationship, health, or wealth. Life has so many dimensions that you should consider when taking stock of what is good, and what is not. When you start applying to every area the same expectations and boundaries, only then will you reap the reward that you are working so hard to obtain.

So yes, many of us need to draft that two-weeks notice memo, and begin preparing to dispose of the negative falsehoods that you have accepted as truths, and eliminate the negative people who have contributed to your own self-defeating behaviors.

Now before I continue to further explain the "Two-Weeks Notice" memo, let me be the first to say that I have not always practiced what I am now preaching. From my previous disclosures, it is painfully clear that I was someone who did not always cancel false friendships or terminate tedious relationships when they were proving themselves a challenge to my own well-being. But with having mentors and reading books such as:

> *Act Like a Success, Think Like a Success* by Steve Harvey;
>
> *The Power Playbook: Rules for Independence, Money, and Success* by LaLa Anthony;
>
> *Essentialism* by Greg McKeown;
>
> *Forgiveness: 21 Days to Forgive Everyone for Everything* by Iyanla Vanzant;
>
> *Abundance Now* by Lisa Nichols; and

Rich Bitch by Nicole Lapin

I decided that it was time for me to be exactly who I was called to be. Therefore, I wrote my "Two-Weeks Notice" memo to the false representative that I had become. I terminated relationships (both intimate and casual) that were making more withdrawals than deposits. I had to cancel my subscriptions to anything that promoted negative energy. I let go of everything that stood in the way of me producing and being the best person that I could be. I started believing that it was IN ME to win, and accepting the fact that I had to LOSE TO WIN. No one wins without some form of a loss, and I was not exempt. I finally took on the "*life goals*" and made my life exactly how I intended for it to be. I finally regained the reins of the runaway carriage that was my life, and brought it to a screeching halt in order to get it back on the road. I went back to being the intent that was meant to be purposed by the name on my birth certificate, instead of acclimating to the other names everyone else called me. I was ready to live in my truth so I gave notice of my intent to change and walked away more liberated than I had ever been before.

Now I know you might be thinking, "Charron, how do I write a "Two-Weeks Notice" memo as it pertains to my life? Well, I am happy you asked! You simply write it just like you would write a resignation letter for your job, but in this letter, you specifically list the things in your life that you need to resign from, never to return, and the reasons these things need to be removed from your life. For example, here is a letter that I wrote:

Date: June 29, 2013

Dear Ms. "Old" Charron Monaye,

I am writing to inform you that I am resigning from my position as being naïve, gullible, and controlled. My resignation will be effective in two weeks so that I can properly plan and prepare for my departure because when I leave, I do not want a reason to return.

I would like to say a special thank you for all that you allowed to happen in my life thus far. All of the experiences with my parents, my relationships, myself, and my peers taught me that I need to now live for me. Your lack of self-worth and dedication to compromising your happiness has me unhappy and truly unfulfilled. The expertise and lessons learned I have developed while being with you has hurt me to a point to where I now only want to feel love. I can no longer give others power over my life or permission to dictate my fate. I want to control my choices and be one with my decisions. I don't care if I win or lose, but that I tried and excelled my way.

I believe this 2 week notice period will be adequate for you to find my replacement (I know misery loves company) and I am not willing to help or train your new fool. Before my departure, I will terminate all relationships and situations that will link me to who you represent. Once these 2 weeks are over, I do not want to recognize my life or the people in it. I am granting myself the ability to replace everything that has caused me hardship and restructure the mindset I've allowed you to keep me on the path to destruction. I appreciate all that you have given me and I promise to make you proud by being the unapologetic one that got away.

I wish you the very best and so honored to be leaving.

Sincerely,
The "New" Charron Monaye

Do you see how detailed I was about what I was resigning from and why? I held myself accountable and told myself what I did wrong and what I desired for myself now. When you own your truth and are able, to be honest with yourself, you discover the person everyone tried to hide from you, by treating you "less than". Now, I challenge you to write your "Two Weeks' Notice" memo to yourself so that you can start the process of eliminating all that is not adding value to your life, and disposing of anything that is preventing you to live with purpose.

Please use the template below and write to your heart's content. The more specific you are in your letter, the more accountable you will be to yourself when you go back to read it, as you should, repeatedly, as a way to bolster your determination to move forward. Start today! Even if you do not finish the letter today, in this moment, start it…NOW!

Date _____
To _____

_____
_____
_____
_____
_____
_____
_____
_____
_____
_____
_____
_____
_____

Sincerely,
YOUR NAME HERE

Now might be a good time for you to take a break, collect your thoughts, give some thought to the things you have just written and how you will begin to execute this letter.

Throughout my entire experience of giving notices, and taking my power back from others who did not deserve it, and becoming acclimated with who I was again, I found my peace within. I was able to restore my ability to live unapologetically, and within my purpose. I have regained my identity, and I know exactly who I am. I have tailored my business to be more about Charron "the author", instead of bringing focus on the other roles I have played such as, the songwriter, the CNN iReport contributor, the playwright, and the publisher. Now don't get me wrong, being in those roles has been fulfilling because they allowed me to expand my writing and help others with the process of getting their voices heard. However, with my rediscovery, I had to lean on my experience and return to the reason why I started writing in the first place. I had to revisit my purpose in life. Was I living my life to benefit myself, or to be that person who worked to benefit others? This is a question we all have to ask ourselves at some point in our lives, because we get so consumed by the task of helping others achieve their goals that we forget to help ourselves. By the time we circle back to paying attention to ourselves, we have lost momentum, lost ground, lost opportunities that we can't get back, and most importantly, we have lost time. As a result, we become bitter, complacent, regretful and angry. We are then holding onto anger directed at others who have drained us, but have not replenished as they have taken from us. Let me tell you something you may already know…"People will only do to you, what you allow", so we can't walk around blaming others for our desires not being fulfilled, we have to blame ourselves for allowing ourselves to forget about our own purpose. Now can you see why the "Two Weeks Notice" memo is so necessary! You can't grow when you have excuses, distractions, or completely impossible expectations of yourself (trying to be super(wo)men) hanging over your head.

Coaching Time:

The first step to owning your life is by ***Acknowledging*** both who and what is hindering you, (if it's you, then acknowledge that too). Next, ***Accepting*** and taking full responsibility for what you did in the experience, whether it is good or bad, and setting forth a plan to execute a new reality and ***Attain*** what it is you want to achieve. So with all of that,

> Are you ready to live life according to the beat of your own drum?
>
> Are you ready to change your mindset, perspective, and thereby change the outcomes in your life?
>
> Are you ready for your promotion to the next level in life?

If you answered yes to these three questions, here are some things you can do to progress towards the goal of being authentically yourself:

Notify the "who" in person ~ Life changing conversation should be discussed via a verbal exchange so that the receiver can fully understand they're being removed and to clarify (if desired) the purpose why.

Avoid Emotional Outbursts ~ Your decision is not at all up for discussion or reconsideration. Do not let a person's use of anger, yelling, or guilt make you feel bad, ashamed, or sorry for being determined, and making changes that are beneficial for you.

Show gratitude for the lessons learned ~ Every person in your life has a reason for being there, even if they are now being removed. Some have brought negative experiences that you can learn from, others may have brought positive resources that will be great tools to apply when necessary, and still some will have had no contribution, good or bad. Regardless of what you have or have not received in the past, be grateful because it will all serve as a stepping stone as you learn what to accept or not accept later on down your road.

When living a purpose driven life, everything you do, and everyone with whom you form an association, has to align with what you are striving to accomplish. Moving forward, I challenge you to be smarter and wiser when allowing people into your universe. If they can't add to your value, then you need to immediately subtract them from the equation. Before we go to the next chapter, let's identify who needs to be served. Remember we can't move forward with baggage, poor judgment, and self-destruction cuffed to our ankles, and expect rewarding and legendary lifestyles. It is time to break the chains.

Who have you identified as needing to receive a "Two Weeks Notice" memo from you so that you can start on the road to living the life you desire?

_____
_____
_____
_____
_____
_____
_____

What baggage are you holding onto that is keeping you complacent?

_____
_____
_____

At what point in your life did you give these negative attributes of life permission to hold you back?

What steps are you going to take in order to take your life back? Please list and rank at least the first 3 steps, in order of importance and describe what is needed to accomplish each step.

Step 1.

Step 2.

Step 3.

LOSE TO WIN

Fantasia has a song that I absolutely love entitled, *"Lose to Win"*, from the *"Side Effects of You"* album. The chorus asks:

Have you ever?Needed someone so bad? But he ain't willing to make it last Sometimes you gotta lose to win again. If it makes you cry, cry, cry And all you do is fight Can't get no sleep at night? Sometimes you gotta lose to win again.

Now look back over your life, and apply those words to your situations. Have you ever needed someone so bad? Have you ever been a part of something in your life that made you cry constantly and all you could do was fight? Have you ever been languishing over something that weighed so heavily on your heart and mind that you couldn't get any sleep at night? What did you lose so that you could regain your sanity? I used to hate losing at life. Losing to me equated failure within myself. Anyone who knows me knows that the word "failure" was my middle name for years. It was nothing for me to say, "I am such a failure" or "I failed again so I might as well quit". I mentally brainwashed myself by believing that I was incapable of success, that I was indeed a complete failure. It became so real to me that I started to live in my conviction. I had the definition of failure memorized! "The condition or fact of not achieving the desired end or ends", and for me, that was the reality that I internalized and used to define myself. Don't get me wrong, I have the ability to accomplish anything, but if there were any deviation, or if anything did not resolve in the manner in which I originally intended, to me, that was a sign of failure. But, when Steve Harvey said, "Failure is God pointing you in a different direction! Don't let failure define you", I opened both ears to hear that again and changed my perspective.

Let's Have an Open and Honest Conversation:

For example, let's circle back to the relationship I spoke about in the last chapter. Family and friends warned me about his intentions, but as a person in love, I did not listen. In spite of everything, I remained loyal, dedicated, and devoted to making him happy, and helping to make his dreams come true. However, after realizing that I had to choose between his dreams and mine, I had to a choice to make. And for some time, I chose his dreams, and allowed mine to fall by the wayside, only to hear him complain, "You don't do anything for me", or, "All you care about is yourself". Instead of me recognizing the error of my ways in remaining with him, I doubled my efforts to make him happy, and worked extra hard hoping he would finally acknowledge and appreciate my hard work. The end result? He left me one month, and a few months later was married to someone else. Now, some may judge me for my decision to remain with him. Believe me, I certainly spent a great deal of time passing judgment on myself so I would not blame you at all. But after losing my first love, ending a marriage, and being cheated on by another, the last thing I wanted was to lose again, even if it meant losing myself to keep him. I have mentioned in my previous books how I labeled myself a failure and held myself solely accountable for my failed relationships. Instead of seeing my value in love, I tried to eliminate the stigma of losing love from my story, and accepted what was given, not realizing that I was losing anyway. But after venting, and seeking guidance from friends and my mother, I saw the victory that was presenting itself in that particular loss, and used that to heal myself, turning my loss to the ultimate win. You see, when we refuse to leave situations that are not intended for us, God makes these situations so unbearable that when something or someone exits your life, you are forced to deal with the real problem…YOU. Believe it or not, God used this man to give me my walking papers, to teach me my own value, and to assist me in regaining my self-worth, and with that my life, even if I was alone. But don't let me mislead you! When he left, I cried like a baby. It hurt me to my core, even though I KNEW even deeper that it was better than what I would have done for myself. I did not understand why he could not see what I was giving him. I could not fathom why he could not recognize that I had given up so much of myself so that he could be happy. I battled against what was best for me, because I had become so entrenched in the negativity. This situation, like many others I had to overcome, taught me that losing the fight is not always a bad thing, especially when you have so much to gain and win down the road. Sometimes, it is very difficult to recognize the win through the pain of whatever battle you are losing. Losing him made me go through a complete restructuring of how I love, live, and laugh at life, and who I allow to participate in the festivities. I had to do a complete 360 degree turn in not just love, but in life in general. I have become very picky and much less tolerant relating to what I will accept from people and life. Not because I am mean or bitter, but because I am ready to win with individuals who are tired of losing, and who are ready to move their mindsets on to brighter things.

Since that loss, I can't express the amount of favor God has showered upon my life. I now have a successful career with my writing. I have a man who loves me, supports me, & motivates me to fulfill MY dreams, and appreciates what I do for him. He truly listens to my heart without me speaking, and more importantly, he allows me into his heart as well. In addition, my sons are at peace and that makes my life the brightest it has ever been. So now, when I sit back and reminisce on the pain of my past, I smile and laugh, because it was in that pain that I learned how to be more compromising without being compromised, balanced without being burdened, loving without being naive, and supportive without being supplanted! Everything in my life right now is exactly how I need it to be, simply because the players involved respect my life, and love me for being resilient and for being able to overcome what could have destroyed me. Things in my life are where I want them to be, simply because I stopped fighting the loss, and allowed it to become my WIN!

In addition to my relationships, let me share with you a professional lesson learned as a result of my own lack of knowledge. This lesson cost me both personally, and financially. I co-produced my first stage play "Living your Life," back in 2011 and I was confident that I was going to sell out every show. I assumed that all of my friends, family, sorority sisters, masonic members, celebrity friends, church friends and co-workers were going to purchase every ticket I had. Because I was so certain of my circles, I decided that it was not necessary to aggressively promote this play. In my estimation, with all of the people I knew, and through all of the organizations that I belonged to, ticket sales would be covered. Was I ever so wrong! Even though I had a great turnout, I did not sell nearly as much as I had assumed. In this instance, I not only failed myself, but also my cast. If I had promoted the play properly, they would have performed to sold out audiences every night, which was my ultimate goal. Afterwards, I told myself that I was never going to produce or write another play, but 2 weeks later I was invited to perform that same play in Washington D.C. the next summer at the D.C. Theater Festival. So what do you think I did? That's right, I took my production down to Washington D.C., but this time around I promoted it fervently, and received the support I knew the play deserved. However, if I had followed my first mind immediately after the first run of the play, I would have given the income loss and the lack of support permission to deter me. Moreover, had I allowed that deterrent, I probably would not be where I am today as a writer and producer. Failure, as I explained in my previous book, "**Love The Real You**", is necessary for anyone to win anything. Failure teaches you how to see life from different perspectives. It is not always your fault that you lose, but it is always your choice to remain entrenched in the situations that occur as a result of the loss. I have at times looked at failure as my punishment for moving in directions that are not of God's will, or being too eager to succeed and losing my humility in the midst of the opportunity. Often, we bring failure upon ourselves, but for some, it is a condition that, if never experienced, would leave important lessons unlearned. I can't say that I would be able to love my man with the openness that I am capable of today, if it was not for the failed relationships before him. If I had not paid the price of surrendering my voice to everyone around me before him, I would not know how to effectively communicate to him my needs and desires today. He is benefitting handsomely as a result of the wins taken from my lessons learned, thus providing us the capability to live and love within a peaceful space that has been created just for us, through our own experiences. What I have found in him is different from anything that I have ever experienced, yet I only arrived here by way of suffering through things that I never believed myself capable of enduring. The same concept holds true with my writing! I would not be comfortable with producing or investing in my work if I had not endured the lack of support and the inevitable loss of money that followed after my first production. That failure taught me that you can not just jump into ANYTHING, whether it be theater, music, or knitting, without first educating yourself on the processes involved, and fully understanding the marketing. In addition, when you are embarking on fulfilling your dreams, you must not assume that family, friends, or organization members are going to support you. You have to learn the industry, hire the right people, and know who your target audience is, which enables you to traverse your journey unbothered, whether or not your circles decide to attend. Today, as a result of many of these "failures turned into wins", I am writing for others, writing for myself, and instead of losing my mind, I am gaining a sense of purpose and becoming comfortable with the truth that writing is not only my calling, but also my gift.

In addition to changing my perception on failure, I had to learn and understand the power of forgiveness. Forgiveness has allowed me to become who it is that I am today. It will help me move on to who it is I will be tomorrow. Forgiving my past, myself, and my failures gave me permission to accept the wins with open arms. I could not have appreciated the favor or mercy granted by God if I was still holding onto the pain and hurt from others and my prior decisions. I had to let it all go. T D. Jakes has a quote that continues to help me daily. He said,

"Unforgiveness denies the victim the possibility of parole and leaves them stuck in the prison of what was, incarcerating them in their trauma and relinquishing the chance to escape beyond the pain."

"Incarcerated in my pain" is where I have lived my life for years. I shackled my hands and feet, imprisoned my mind, and most of the time, by my own doing as opposed to the torment of others. Now, when I read Iyanla Vanzant, "Forgiveness: 21 Days to Forgive Everyone for Everything", her words set me free and made me acknowledge that it was time to give myself the permission to forgive so that I can continue living. As Iyanla says,

"Only forgiveness can liberate minds and hearts once held captive by anger, bitterness, resentment, and fear. Forgiveness is a true path to freedom that can renew faith, build trust, and nourish the soul."

Forgiveness doesn't mean agreeing with, condoning or even liking what has happened. Forgiveness means letting go and knowing that—regardless of how challenging, frightening, or difficult an experience may seem—everything is just as it needs to be in order for you to grow and learn. When you focus on how things "should" be, you deny the presence and power of love. The ability to accept the events of the past, while being willing to change your perspective on them, will move you into the season of winning. This is why we must change our mindsets regarding the concept of "losing" and acknowledge the rewards that lie within the experience! Allow me to share the lyrics of another song that embodies the "Lose to Win" concept. This song, by Daniel Powter, suggests that, "Losing to win is a difficult requirement, but there is joy within the journey:

You wake up in the morning
But the story is the same as before
You're looking in the mirror
But you just don't see yourself anymore
So give up what you know,
What you learned and what you're all about
As long as you don't give up on you
Then you can find your way out...

It don't take any money, don't take nothing but what you have inside
It doesn't matter if you fall down
It only counts if you try...
So pull the blinds and let the light shine through
Don't you think it's time for the light
To finally shine right on you...

So let them know what's underneath it all...
You won't fall
And baby you'll move mountains too
There is nothing really left for you to prove
'Cause everybody knows you lose before you win
And if you're finally at the end of your rope
Well then you just begin
When the world feels like it's left you behind
Just get back up and you will find
Everybody knows in the end you got to lose just to win...

As you can see, I glean many of life's lessons from music. That is simply because music has the capability of being the universal language that teaches us, heals us, and redirects us to a more positive place. Have you ever turned on the radio, while in a bad mood, and your favorite song comes on and instantly you feel good? If you have, then you understand why I turn to music as another form of therapy and coaching. When it comes to losing to win, remember you have to understand that you need one to fully appreciate the other. The things we tend to cherish the most are those for which we have set forth some type of struggle. Heartbreak is often attached to those things that we desire the most. Here are some tips on appreciating your failures so that you can see the victory and obtain the favor that God has on the other side for you.

Failure Reveals Our Strength and Ability ~ My son who is a member of the Civil Air Patrol (Auxiliary to the United States Air Force) says, "Pain is weakness leaving the body", meaning that sometimes in order to become stronger, we will need to feel the pain that occurs as the feeble places are tested. Failure shows the areas that need to be improved or strengthened. Failure presents the opportunity to show if you have the strength to push through the weakness, and it will show if you have the ability to correct the weakness, and thereby eradicate the failure. As long as your emotional pain does not destroy you, it will eventually make you stronger, if you allow it to do so. Failure is ultimately pain that builds you up, or hopelessness that tears you down. The road that you choose will determine if you break, or if you heal and get stronger in your journey.

Failure Inspires Others ~ There is a saying, "God can turn any mess into a message, any test into a testimony"! When you look at what you've been through and compare it to those in the world around you, you are bound to run into someone who will need your inspiration and guidance. We have all lived a life, and have struggled to overcome many of the same things. The only difference is, we all arrive and overcome at different times. We should be encouraged to share our testimonies, and be open to receive insight shared from others as well. There may be a message within their story that may give life to a new opportunity or action necessary to turn your situation around. You will never have a legacy without first facing a challenge.

Failure Builds Courage ~ When you are faced with failure, you exercise the muscles of courage and faith, and as these muscles gain strength, they make you more determined and eager to win. Have you ever run a race and found yourself trailing behind someone who is focused and heading to the finish line? Did your realization that you were about to lose awaken in you a sense of renewed determination? Did you feel the adrenaline running through you, making you push even harder? Did you realize that you were sweating, breathing heavily, and moving faster than you ever have before? You surprised yourself by pushing past your normal limits, and even if you did not win the actual race, you pulled through at the end to FINISH. In this situation, you did not win the physical race, but the figurative victory is yours. You built your stamina in the face of the loss of the race. You increased your courage and improved your faith in yourself because you surpassed your own limits. Your win was in the finish and in the confidence that finishing established within your heart, whether first or last. Failure often serves as a vehicle to increase your capacity to believe in yourself, even if you are the only one who does.

Failure is Better than Regret ~ Marvin Sapp once shared something so profound to me, that it resonates with me still: "A friend of mine said something powerful at his grandfather's funeral. He said that the greatest lesson from his grandfather's life was that he died empty, because he accomplished everything he wanted, with no regrets. I think that, along with leaving a legacy, would be the greatest sign of success." When you live life the way, you desire and with your own voice, you tend to appreciate and respect the process of living. Never deny yourself the right to live out of fear of regretting the outcome. Denying yourself the opportunity to accomplish, as a result, of fear is failing in itself because you did not try. Always give yourself permission to attempt to either secure the win or learn the lesson. Trying and failing is better than regretting that you never tried at all. Regrets will always keep you guessing.... "What If...?"

Failure Brings Resilience ~ Have you ever stretched a rubber band as wide as it could go, and then released it? What happened to the piece of rubber? Once the tension released, the rubber band returned to its original shape and form. It didn't just sidle back into its original shape, it SNAPPED back! At times, failure, or losing, can place so much tension on us, that we feel, overwhelmed and stretched to the point of breaking. However, when that tension is removed, just like that snappy rubber band, know that we will return to our original shape, perhaps with a new direction and a renewed sense of purpose. In Lisa Nichols' book, "No Matter What", she shares the importance of understanding your "bounce-back muscles", and how they give you the strength and agility you need to navigate life's speed bumps. Being resilient in the face of failure allows you to recover more quickly, and prepares your mind for the rebuilding of your confidence during your storm. Resilience allows you to stand for something, even when you have every reason to fall. Resilience is the seed that once planted, springs forth to motivate you to believe in yourself and move forward towards your win.

Ultimately, the power of "losing to win" lies in your ability to trust yourself, in being comfortable with standing alone, and in being fearless when it comes to pissing off some people. The power behind making your failures into your wins lies in your ability to remain true to yourself. Do you trust yourself enough to know that you have the ability to carry yourself the full distance required to reach your finish line? Is it a book, a relationship, a career move, or life experience that you are holding yourself back from because you don't trust yourself? Are you holding yourself back out of fear of losing? Are you skipping steps in your journey, hoping to prevent failure from showing its ugly face? If these questions sound like you, allow me to be the first to tell you to STOP!!! You are hustling backwards and moving nowhere fast. You are walking in circles, wishing on the big payback. But your payback will only come through once you understand the full process, commit yourself unconditionally, and being willing to accept the risks that are inherent. Life is full of situations in which the only thing you have to lose is the opportunity to try. Sometimes you win, sometimes you lose, but the joy of it all is knowing that you tried, and survived to talk about it, whether to your girlfriends over tea, or to a room full of people at a conference.

Never be afraid to live life authentically and without reservation. The day you put your guard down and live, will be the day you allow failure and losing to be repurposed into the catalysts that launch you to your ultimate goal. Take a closer look at me! I had to lose money, love, my faith, and my career before I realized that losing them was not the end of my world but the beginning of appreciating them more. Appreciate the losses, so you can secure the wins. The things that you desire in life lives on the other side of failure, but only the risk-takers who are both determined and focused, have any chance at all to win the race. Les Brown has a quote that keeps me motivated to push forward and secure my wins, no matter the trial, obstacle, or heartbreak.

"The graveyard is the richest place on earth, because it is here that you will find all the hopes and dreams that were never fulfilled, the books that were never written, the songs that were never sung, the inventions that were never shared, the cures that were never discovered, all because someone was too afraid to take that first step, keep with the problem, or determined to carry out their dream." ~ Les Brown

It is better to live life to the fullest, so that when you perish you can die in peace and empty.

After reading the previous section, think about what fears you are holding onto, why you might be afraid of losing, and what wins are you ready to receive. Consider these things and list them below:

What fears are you holding onto....

_____
_____
_____
_____
_____
_____

What circumstances or situations make you afraid of losing?

_____
_____
_____
_____
_____
_____

What wins are you ready to receive?

_____
_____
_____
_____
_____
_____

Is there anyone who is hindering you from starting/finishing the race to meet goals in your life? Who might they be?

_____
_____
_____
_____
_____
_____

Why would the people you listed above still be present in your life if you are able to identify them as deterrents?

_____
_____
_____
_____
_____
_____

What is your biggest fear about letting go? Why are you afraid of this outcome?

_____
_____
_____
_____
_____
_____

PERSONAL OWNERSHIP

In the first chapter, we acknowledged that it is time to give some "Two Week Notices" to those people and things that are deterring us from living the life that will fulfill our needs, desires, and dreams. In the second chapter, we acknowledged the importance of understanding that losses are essential to the journey of life, and how critical it is for us to learn to accept these losses as lessons, instead of road blocks.

In this chapter, you will begin the process of taking personal ownership of your story. Together, we will explore your mistakes, and own them. You will work on being able to acknowledge what YOU did wrong, so that YOU can address it head on, in order to prevent YOU from failing to attain the freedom you seek to receive by the end of this book. I will warn you now, I may step on your figurative toes, and perhaps stomp on my own toes in the process. We never like to turn the hand around and point the finger in our own direction when it comes to addressing the decisions we have made, and the ensuing consequences of those decisions. To you, my dearest readers, class is now in session, and it is time to take ownership of your faults, your attitude, and your life. YES!, I said attitude, because you would be surprised by how much your attitude affects your view on life, and how it impact your overall mindset.

Before we begin the journey of taking accountability for ourselves, please answer the following coaching questions. Allow me to open your mind to receive the information that is soon to be given.

My life feels most fulfilled when I....
_____
_____

The most difficult vice that I am unwilling or afraid to give up is…

The reason why I should live my life for me is…

The best way to describe who I am is….

The best way to describe why I feel that I am here is…

_____
_____
_____
_____
_____
_____

They say the first step to recovering or healing is simply to by acknowledge that you either "have a problem" or "you need help". Unfortunately, last time I checked, most humans are not mind readers and therefore are not able to decipher what you need and when you need it. They can not tell you what is right or wrong for you, if you don't at first initiate the conversation to seek guidance. Acknowledging that you are not in charge of your life is the first step towards your liberation. You should not have to ask anyone for permission to live your life the way you desire, but you do have to know what it is that you desire in order to be living your life for yourself.

__Action moment__: I want you to take an inventory of your life as it is today to determine how much of your OWN life, YOU actually own. Take a moment to consider the following questions and answer them honestly:

In the space of a week, how much of your time would you say is spent doing what you want versus doing what others want you to do for them? Can you list specific examples?

_____
_____

How much of your time is spent taking steps towards fulfilling your dreams versus planning and building someone else's dream? Can you list specific examples?

How often in the course of a week will you sacrifice something that you want or need, in order to provide someone else with something that they want? Can you list specific examples?

How many times within the last month have you felt frustrated or angry about not being able to accomplish something that you set out to do? Can you list specific examples? For each example please list WHY the task was not accomplished.

_____
_____
_____
_____
_____
_____

Now, look back over your answers. Based on what you wrote, can you honestly say that YOU really own YOU? From the time you wake up in the morning to the time you go to sleep, how much of your day is spent accomplishing anything you want for yourself? Does it almost feel like a chore to pencil your own needs into YOUR day, in order to complete at least one task that will benefit you? Being a mother, girlfriend, best friend, employee, daughter, sister, sorority sister, O.E.S sister, and entrepreneur, very seldom do I have time left in my day to do anything of interest to me, except go to sleep, or watch Scandal or The Braxtons. This kind of life has made me miss appointments, opportunities, and networking events that had the ability to enhance my life or business. Thus, I had to become just as devoted to myself, as I was to everyone else whose needs seemed to be much more important than my own. I facilitated this newly found devotion to ME by deciding to grant myself vacation days from my everyday life. Vacation days from your life, allows you that time off to do everything that YOU want. Imagine waking up in peace, not having to cater to anyone but yourself, and having the liberty to go and come without being needed by someone else. You are enjoying your life and embracing the moments experienced within the time alone. You are enjoying the opportunity to focus on meeting your needs. Vacations are exciting to everyone! Vacations from life should be just as exciting. It may be a new concept, but it is a phenomenal one, and should be implemented with as much frequency as possible. Today, I challenge you to look at your schedule and pick 2 weekends that you will devote completely to yourself. This time "away" truly helped me to begin my owning process and taught me how to balance my time and energy when it comes to being everything to everybody, but nothing to myself. Being nothing to myself was the reason why it was so easy to unwittingly give my life away, and then have to ask permission to get it back. When you give people the keys to drive your journey, you never know where you will end up and nine times out of ten, allowing others to drive your journey will not get you to where you want to go.

Owning your life is essential to truly knowing WHO you are, WHERE you are going, and WHY you make certain decisions that ultimately affect your lifestyle and dreams. You will never be able to arrive at your final destination in life if you don't first own the right to make the decisions to get you there. Personal ownership is your only way to acknowledge what you want, be prepared to accept what you have to do to get it, and appreciate the journey required to maintain it. Personal ownership will also move you to a frame of mind where you are not only able to take responsibility for the decisions that have brought you to this place in your life, but you are also ready to be committed to taking action toward resolving challenges that you have identified as barriers to your personal success. Once you are able to take responsibility for your life and own the decisions made, only then will you be able to give notice to anyone that you have now officially arrived. You can't take ownership and ask for permission at the same time, thus you are left to decide which side of the fence you want to be on. Some people have a hard time making those difficult decisions, and require the assistance of someone who will hint, nudge, or maybe even all out shove them in the direction that they should be going, and what they should be doing to get where they need to be.

Just as some people are unable to accept the idea of facing the responsibility that they are the reason why their lives are dysfunctional or not going as planned, there are others who put all of their energy into blaming, complaining, and finding fault in others, instead of themselves. For example, when I was a paralegal working in employment, personal injury and criminal law, a common reason for the cases presented was that, "my employer fired me for no reason at all". Being educated in employment law, I know that the employment-at-will doctrine gives employers the right to terminate an employee at any time, for any reason (except an illegal one), or, for no reason at all, without incurring legal liability. Likewise, an employee is free to leave a job at any time, for any or no reason, with no adverse legal consequences. However, every client that came into the office was filing wrongful termination suits, claiming that they were "fired for no reason". Eventually, you have to ask them, "Is there anything that you may have done to contribute to the decision by your employer". No one wanted to confess his or her role or what he or she might have done that led to the firing. They all sat in the boardroom; innocent and victimized, until the employer's attorney provided my attorney exhibits of excessive lateness, stealing, assault, or coming to work intoxicated. As soon as the clients were questioned about the allegations, we heard stuttering and excuses, and I was given the cue to create the invoice to bill the client for wasting our time. There were occasions when we had clients who were wrongfully terminated or had every right to sue based on negligence, but were few and far in between. After comparing the number of true victims versus those who refused to take ownership in their termination, lead us to draw the conclusion that people are more concerned with blaming others to make themselves feel better, instead of accepting their role and responsibility in the situation. Now, I understand that getting fired from a job is devastating, but owning your role in the termination and growing from it will not only help you to accept the separation like a mature adult, it will help you learn from your mistakes. You never know, that termination could be the start of something better; however, an avoidant attitude could cause you to miss any possible opportunities before they could actually happen, especially if you approached it still blaming the prior employer for their decision. When you take responsibility for your life, you own the power to move forward.

As stated above, personal ownership is not only you taking responsibility for your life and your decisions, but also for the consequences that come from those decisions. We have to learn how to say, "Yes, I did that and I am going to do better" or, "Yes, I own my part in the situation and I apologize". Say it and mean it! Mean it when you say it! If you don't stand up, and do so with authenticity, who will ever take you seriously. Own your decisions and believe in yourself enough to know that your choice is, was, or will be beneficial for you or those you love. This is also true for your mistakes and failures; you would not know how to do better if you do not know what didn't work. Trust me, there will be people who will disagree with you, ridicule your thinking, call you names, or stop talking to you because of your choices, and because you make decisions and abide by them. You have to know that doing what is pleasing for you is the fastest way to losing those that would prefer that you did what was better for them. For some, the thought of losing others for their own happiness is a choice that is difficult to make. So when faced with the choice to cut them or keep them, I have to ask, aren't you worthy of being happy and true to yourself? Isn't it about time that you stand up for your life and do with it, as you will? Deciding to become a writer, and essentially gambling with my kid's lives financially, I often had people challenge my decision to continue on this journey. Questioning my decision to spend money to pursue a dream that did not always offer guaranteed returns, often made me reconsider my decision to write. However, my determination and commitment to my craft kept me wealthy and rich in ways that I never expected, and the hardships that the naysayers predicted did not materialize. Owning my career and decision made some people angry, however, I have learned that just like anything else, they would get over it. Deciding to own your life, or remain a visitor in your own world, is completely up to you. However, I am here to tell you that being an active participant in the one life you have is more rewarding than sitting around dreaming about the life you desire. It is definitely more rewarding than allowing others to dictate what you do in your own life. Your decision, or refusal to decide, to actively make the moves to own what is yours is the only thing that is stopping you from receiving what is ultimately ordained for you.

As I stated before, my decision to own my life, my love, and my happiness was the beginning of my receiving the life, the love, and the happiness I have prayed for. God was not giving me what I was praying for because I was not learning, owning, or taking responsibility for my share of the decisions I made in my life. Instead of labeling myself a failure all those years, I should have labeled myself a human. Instead of blaming the failure of every relationship on the man, I had to look deep within and own my part. I had to look at myself and find the blemishes and imperfections that made me behave the way that I did. I had to identify what was unpleasing and readjust my personality, behaviors, reactions, and conversations to fit the reality of the person that I wanted to be. I had to change the life I knew, and create the story I wanted to be remembered by. That change not only gave me hope, it gave me a sense of purpose.

I hope that what I am saying is making sense to you and motivating you to take responsibility for your life. I hope that you are inspired to stop living a life that is unrecognizable to you. You owe it to yourself to live the life you want, and reap the rewards you desire. To further help you see how accepting personal responsibility and ownership of your life is beneficial to your overall existence, here are a few points that highlight the importance of ownership:

> **Freedom:** By accepting personal responsibility, you gain the freedom to accept your decisions, make your own choices, create your own life, and feel free to live it the way that you choose.
>
> **Stop Making Excuses:** Making excuses is similar to blaming others, except it involves blaming circumstances instead of people.

Recognize Your Choices: At any given time and in any given situation, you have a choice of how to respond. Own your ability and responsibility in making those choices.

Accept Yourself and Your Circumstances: Accept responsibility for who you are right now. Accept the circumstances that your choices have brought you to. Recognize that it's not others who have made you the way you are, but only you.

Stop Relying On External Validation: Don't depend on other people to make you feel good about yourself. If you depend on external validation to be happy, you abdicate your personal responsibility for your own life and your own happiness.

You Are Not Responsible for Other People: Accepting personal responsibility involves letting go of the need to feel responsible for others.

"Accept responsibility for your own life. Remember, it is you who will get you to where you want to be. Take the time to look at where you are and ask yourself the following questions;

"Did I make an appointment with myself to be here? What part of myself do I need to let go of in order to facilitate the move forward into the next chapter in my life?" Hold yourself to a higher standard and know that you hold the key to your own future! You have GREATNESS within you!!" ~ Les Brown

THE 3 A'S
Acknowledge, Acceptance, Attainment

ACKNOWLEDGE: "The proactive approach to a mistake is to acknowledge it instantly, correct and learn from it." — Stephen Covey

Definitions:
Accept or admit the existence or truth of.
Recognize the fact or importance or quality of.

ACCEPTANCE: "Understanding is the first step to acceptance, and only with acceptance can there be recovery." — J.K. Rowling

Definitions:
The action of consenting to receive or undertake something offered.
The action or process of being received as adequate or suitable

ATTAINMENT: "To begin to think with purpose, is to enter the ranks of those strong ones who only recognize failure as one of the pathways to attainment." — James Allen

Definitions:
The action or fact of achieving a goal toward which one has worked.
A thing achieved, especially a skill or educational achievement.

I know you may be wondering why I start the chapter with definitions and quotes. When it comes to learning new concepts, sometimes we have to understand what the concepts mean, and apply effective affirmations or quotes to engage our thought processes, making it easier for us to develop and understand the concepts in question. Even though those words are relatively easy to figure out, providing more insight will only help you better understand why these words are important for your notices, and how executing each one will enable you to obtain, and then maintain, the life you desire. Your deliverance to happiness depends on your decision to choose to put yourself first, and own the life that you live in every day. My goal for writing this book was to assist you in becoming aware, and provide actionable dialogue to get you thinking and implementing what I call, "The Road to Unapologetic Happiness". As you have read in this book, and in my previous books, I have had my share of ups and down, heartbreaks, setbacks, and obstacles, that have made me want to give up on myself. But my faith in God, the inspiration from my children, and the love from my family made me stay in the race and re-evaluate how I acknowledge my situations, accept myself as a result of those situations, and celebrate the reward of attaining what was mine within those situations. They say, "Life is 10% what happens to you and 90% how you react to it". I learned that my reaction to situations was what hindered me, and the reason that I never maintained anything.

Acknowledge

Before I became sanctified and filled with happiness and love, I was miserable and a people pleaser. I lived my life to make others happy and maintain what I mistakenly believed to be the concept of family. I would sacrifice my finances and life just to ensure that everyone else around me wanted for nothing, and always had everything they needed. Moreover, I compromised my own identity in order to become what others wanted and needed from me, leaving me lost and empty more often than not. Imagine, being asked questions about yourself and not being able to answer them because you have been reprogrammed to reflect whom others needed you to be. This way of living was dark and depressing for me. I would smile to hide the tears while praying daily to find the real me. I can remember being asked the question, "Who are you?", and I laughed to keep from crying because I could not answer honestly. However, it was through coaching and numerous conversations with Author Vaughn McNeill and his challenges that I learned to accept and acknowledge myself. He judged my decisions and provoked stern dialogue that often made me want to run and hide, not because he was wrong, but because I was ashamed of how I gave so many people so much power over my happiness. But then I learned that I cannot depend on others to validate or define my life or happiness, I must do that for myself. After letting that concept digest and attach itself to my spirit, we collectively penned the book, **Love the Real You,** where I used what Vaughn taught, along with my own revelations, and coached myself to who I am today. It was through that process that I learned how to accept myself unconditionally (flaws and all), and own my life unapologetically (sorry, not sorry). Nevertheless, before I could fully accept myself, I had to back track and first acknowledge those setbacks and mistakes that made me feel unworthy. I had to acknowledge that in spite of those "dips", I WAS worthy to have the life I wanted and the happiness I dreamed of. I had to change my mindset and constantly tell myself, "You deserve it". I had to give myself permission to believe that it was okay for me to live my life without the help and/or opinions of others. As my mom would say, "take away the meat and throw away the bone", and I had to learn to do just that. As I started incorporating my discovery of acknowledging myself in my life and owning my decision, I was faced with opposition from those who were used to altering and controlling my thinking. Before this revelation, I would give in more than I would fight back just to keep the peace, because I am not a confrontational person. Anyone who knows me knows that I will run from confrontation or back down and give you your way when pressured. However, writing a book on loving the real you and helping others uncover deficiencies that hinder their process made me find the strength to uncover my own. Realizing that I was not walking and talking according to the expectations that I was encouraging others to live by, I had to re-evaluate my life, which in turn made me take the words that I am writing more seriously. I had to pick a side and become committed to the journey. For once, I had to take my own advice! I made clear that the new life I wanted was more important to me than worrying about, and making peace with people who used intimidation and manipulation as ways to control me. That life had to be buried and as I started speaking up on my own behalf, and no longer caring about the feelings and opinions of others. Those that could not accept the new me soon stopped dealing with me, and with many, my "No's" were met with attitude and silence.

At first, it bothered me that people would rather remove themselves from my life than respect the changes that I needed to make in my life to better things for myself, and accept me for the person I wanted to be. Eventually, I had to recognize and give God praise for removing the negativity from my life, and I bothered no more. You see, the fastest way to learn who's in your corner, is by changing how you treat them, or how you allow them to treat you. True friends will never hurt you, nor will they try to manipulate you in order to better things for themselves. I realized that it was time to clean house. Little did I know, changing how I allowed people to treat me, made them leave on their own. Look at God!!! Living is easy when God removes those who serve no valuable purpose to you, without you having to lift a finger. Every day I took back a piece of my life, a piece of my happiness, and a piece of my will to continue on this journey of writing, all the while, I was being reintroduced to life on my terms. I gradually affirmed my importance and accepted that I am perfectly imperfect and worthy of so much more than I had acquired. Each morning, before I left the house, I would say the following affirmations, just to feed myself with love and life, and as a constant reminder that I do matter to me:

> I love myself unconditionally and accept myself as I am.
> I accept that to err is human and I forgive myself for all my mistakes.
> I am proud of myself and all that I have accomplished.
> I recognize the divinity within me. I respect myself and treat myself with kindness and love.
> I accept myself for what I am and I am constantly trying to better myself.
> I am a valuable person and I try to be as useful to as possible to those around me.
> I am worthy and so is everybody else. I love all.
> As a human being, I have both strengths and weaknesses.
> I love myself and I love the world. I know that love is everything.
> I am my own best friend. I am also a friend to the world.

As I would say these affirmations to myself every day, I felt myself releasing all of the negative phrases and letting go of the constant blame to which I had been subjecting myself for years. Between the criticism and negative words I heard from others, and the self-sabotaging I inflicted, I was teetering on the brink of a nervous breakdown. However, it was in the words of the affirmations above that, I found my strength to hold on and remain steadfast in my transformation period. Along with the affirmations, I completely changed my lifestyle; from what I did, to who I considered a friend, down to how I dressed and wore my hair. I remember one day coming home from work and throwing out the majority of the clothes that were in my closet. Not because I couldn't fit them, but because I wanted to change my appearance, which in turn would change how I felt about myself. For example, I typically wore a lot of black, however, with my new journey, I wanted to add some brightness and color. For that to happen, everything had to go, even my shoes. I made sure that nothing in my life was a deterrent to my goal, and that everything in my life was a representation of what I wanted. I had to become non-negotiable about my life that I went to extreme measures to get to that point. The best part about this transformation was that I did not tell anyone. I did not ask for permission. I did not have a need to go shopping with anyone; or to obtain someone else's opinion as to what I should buy or not buy. I made the decision and moved forward towards change, all by myself. It was at that point that I did not only own my lifestyle and mindset, I owned my whole existence. I became unapologetic about my decisions, and I moved according to my own beat in my new life.

After reading the chapter above, what can you identify as needing to change in your life?

___
___
___
___
___
___
___

Are you ready to acknowledge your faults so that you can learn and grow from them?
Why or why not?

___
___
___
___
___
___
___
___

What do you need to do in your life that will fully liberate you?

_____
_____
_____
_____
_____
_____
_____

I really love the following things about myself....

_____
_____
_____
_____
_____
_____

Acceptance

Lisa Nichols has a quote that changed my perception about the concept of acceptance and how I was trying to obtain it:

"I have nothing to hide
I have nothing to protect
I have nothing to prove
I have nothing to defend"

After saying this quote repeatedly, I began to accept and love being real, raw, and unfiltered. I embraced my vulnerability and lifted my voice, allowing it to be heard and properly understood. I gave myself permission to be me! This was the best thing I could have done for myself! I looked myself in the mirror and I opened my heart to the possibility of what was to come as a result of my determination to change. I created the life I wanted. I became the peace I desired and I loved myself the way I deserved to be loved. I removed the complications and opened myself up to receive what God had in store for me. I surrendered my life by giving him total control, while keeping up with my end of the deal. You see, God can direct us to our greater good, but we have to first be mentally, emotionally, and physically prepared to receive it. As they say, "actions without works is dead". My new journey of living my life depended on my acting and executing, while growing and exploring, which was everything I had always denied myself. As my confidence and self-esteem grew, and my inner being filled with love, I became more and more accepting of my own choices and needs. I no longer compromised my heart for the betterment of others. This time around, I made my needs the primary focus that drove the vessel that propelled me forward. I stopped needing people to accept me or approve of me. I gave myself enough love and care that as long as I was accepting of my own life, everyone else's opinion was a non-factor. I exercised within myself enough confidence and motivation, that my excitement and purpose regarding my decisions was enough for me. I didn't need to notify anyone for validation. I had to learn that everyone does not need to know your every move, thus giving them no room for unsolicited and unnecessary input. The less other people know, the less chance there is for them to implant their negativity or throw shade on your desires. There was no need to consult with others about things that directly affect my life. At the end of the day, I was the only one who was forced to embrace the successes or consequences that came along with whatever decisions I made. When I removed the outside noise, it became easier for me to "do me".

"Doing me" helped me to accept the raw and ugly truths, as well as to be proud of the great and bright moments of my life. It helped me to learn who I am and what I like to do. It also helped me to accomplish things that I had previously delayed, and it enabled me to understand how to maintain my happiness. For so many years, I cheated myself out of being happy. When you live your life focused on pleasing others, you block your own happiness and peace. As a result, I looked around and reviewed what was important to me. I found my happiness in my children, my relationships, and my writing. It was very seldom that I was genuinely happy. Even rarer that I was in control of my happiness, because as soon as someone did something to get under my skin, my happiness was gone. People used to tell me, "no one should be able to change your mood like that". I agreed, but when your happiness is borrowed according to the whims of others, it is just that much easier to lose. Thus, the reason that finding my own happiness during this change was imperative to the success of this transformation. I did not want to be dependent on anyone ever again for anything that I am personally responsible for, and perfectly capable of, providing for myself. I cannot expect someone else to love me if I don't love myself. And I can't expect someone else to be happy with me, if I am not happy with myself. Accepting and acknowledging who I am took a lot of time, but it created results that have left me in a constant state of euphoria. I still say my affirmations on a daily basis, which allows me to maintain my confidence, and continue to heighten my value. Simultaneously, I also did the work within that lessened my vulnerability to outside influences, but kept me available to receive. Here are a few things I did to further assist me with accepting my past, my authentic future, and myself.

1. I learned to appreciate the "imperfect" actions or thoughts that make me Charron Monaye.

2. I made peace with and forgave my past decisions so that I could learn from the mistakes and enhance my future with the lessons that I learned.

3. I had to learn what I wanted out of life while making clear and honest what I was no longer willing to accept.

4. I gave myself permission to be vulnerable and forthcoming with the important truths about who I am, what I have seen, and where I want to go.

5. I allowed myself permission to become human in the eyes of those who usually saw me as a "superwoman". It wasn't easy to reveal this truth to others, however I realized that my truths and my story would be able to encourage others to accept themselves and follow their own dreams.

When you learn to accept who you are, you are better equipped to give the world instructions on how to accept and respect you. This is one of the reasons why accepting your setbacks and learning from your losses is vital. These lessons provide you with the foundation and establish the standards that you need to implement for yourself, now that you have made the decision to give notice. You can't give notice without coming to an understanding regarding the things that took you through struggles and storms. Accepting who I am now, and understanding what I will or will not tolerate, is a direct result of what I endured and had to overcome in my past. My past helped me to learn about all that I did not want, and was no longer willing to accept. Opening myself to the lessons of the past helped me make decisions and prepare for everything I now realize that I actually want. Losing before has now allowed me to win, and that is a priceless gift. Now please understand, I know that I am not finished with losing, but now I will be able to make the choice of learning lessons with each inevitable loss. I chose to acknowledge what I have allowed, and accept the lessons that come with the choices that I have made. Nothing can happen if I don't first accept the action. What are some things that you might need to identify and accept about yourself? What are some things that you may need to change about yourself? Think about those questions as you answer the following coaching questions:

List some imperfections that you are able to identify about yourself?

___
___
___
___
___
___
___

What are some things you are aware of about yourself, but have been hiding from others?

___
___
___
___
___
___
___

What are 3 things that you are ready to confess about yourself that no one knows?

_____
_____
_____
_____
_____
_____
_____

Attainment

Now that we have acknowledged who we are and have refocused on where we desire to go, it will soon be time to celebrate all of our hard work. Yay!!!! Turn Up!!!! Attainment is the moment of culmination, where we celebrate the journey and the goals we set forth for ourselves, and the moment when we actually reach those goals. Changing our mindset is a goal of action, one that demands a lot of mental and emotional readjusting, which requires you to take long, deep breaths after each milestone, and literally pass out at the end of the road. Moving to a place in our lives where we "stop asking for permission", was the goal for us, and as we peeled back layers of ourselves to find the answers to our internal questions, and understand the feelings and emotions that were holding us back, we deserve a minute to sip our wine and let our hair down. Did you expect that you would learn so much about yourself when you purchased this book? Let's toast to education! Did you know that being committed to acknowledging and accepting yourself as the human being that you are, would open up a world of peace and abundance? Let's toast to imperfections leading to strengths. Did you ever really believe that joy truly DOES come in the morning? Let's tap twice and toast to praise. There is always a rainbow on the other side of a storm, but we have to know that we are strong enough, wise enough, and simply *enough* to make it through that storm to peaceful waters.

My journey to attain what I fought so hard to recognize that I deserved had its rough patches, but I made it because of my ability to own *myself,* and by giving notices where they were needed. I can now say that my skies are brighter, and the beat in my heart sings a smooth jazz melody. I can now move through life without being fettered by the cares of the world around me. From my career, to my finances, to my love life, to my health, I am in a much better place simply because I demanded the return of my control. I revised my actions to align with my new goals. I stopped giving money away, and instead worked my way to an excellent credit score! So much so that I was eventually approved for what I always considered to be my dream credit card. I stopped accepting expenses for everyone else's career and life issues, and instead started and maintained a growing savings account. *#Won'tHeDoIt!!* I stopped giving away my time freely, and instead gave myself more vacations away from the toils of life. I was not able to reverse all that I had already given away, but in my planning, I was able to recoup those losses, and use them to do the things that I always wanted to do. However, the biggest reward I was able to gain for myself, was reconnecting with, and mending the love that I allowed to walk away years ago. When you are able to own your mistakes, it is so much easier for you to say "I'm sorry", but when your apology is met with, "I Love You", you are able to sip, toast and dance the night away! Finally, everything I prayed for was being shown to me, and it made the last fifteen years well worth every minute. I am truly living a breathtaking life!! Now that I am giving notices or nothing at all, I feel a complete sense of calm in my writing, confidence in my decisions, and definitive in the way I deal with people. I am no longer defensive or aggressive in either my attitude or emotions, simply because I found that there is no gain in constant turmoil. There is more peace and elegance when you set yourself amongst the clouds and within the sun, so I decided to shine brightly. Now let's be clear, this transformation did not happen overnight, nor did it take a year, or even two…it is a constant process that is always evolving, and presents new blessings every day. When I think back to the start of this journey, I must say thank you to those who pushed me, either by serving as mentors, or by pushing me to my breaking point. Thank you to those who offered a shoulder for me to lean on in my struggle, and to those who were the reason that those offered shoulders were needed. Thank you to those who inspired and motivated me back to life and to the new life that I often wrote about. This journey was not planned, nor was it prepared for. It was something that needed to occur if I wanted to live. Now, don't misunderstand me, I was not suicidal or otherwise endangering myself, but I *was* heavily stressed and endured numerous panic attacks. I was on medication that had me feeling and looking like a zombie. If you did not know any better, you would have thought I was a character from the show "The Walking Dead". It was scary for myself and my children. They had been forced to live with the repercussions of what came from ME not living my life. Their unhappiness and fear of losing me was the catalyst that made me decide that enough was enough. Stress is often determined to be a contributing factor for many deaths or illnesses, and I refused to allow anyone else's foolishness to be the contributing factor in my demise. As a result of my health, my emotional labeling, my financial instability, and the way I had been allowing people to treat me, I was forced to set several goals and implemented several plans, from A, to B, all the way down to whatever letter combination spelled SUCCESS. These plans were set forth to reverse the unhealthy norm that had taken over my home.

Setting goals and implementing actionable plans are the most important steps when it comes to fully owning your life. As you begin to acknowledge and accept your past, and own your right to your future, you will then be challenged to decide what your tomorrow will look like and how long it will take you to get there. This is when being honest in your truth, and realistic in your revelations, plays the biggest part. Transforming your life is never going to be a "hit it and quit it" kind of job. It will be full of elements and areas that will constantly require your attention. When you think about your life as a whole, you have to examine all that is in that life, that makes up the person you are. What are your everyday responsibilities? What do you expect to accomplish in your day-to-day life? In my opinion, we have eight areas within our lives that intertwine consistently, and require our attention if we expect them to function properly. These following areas impact us daily:

> **Spiritual** ~ this area includes our faith and belief in a spiritual being that is greater than ourselves. This where we find our strength, and build on the belief that we can do all things.
>
> **Physical** ~ this area includes our health and physical wellness. Our body is what we need to be fully functional and alive in this world. It is essential that you take care of your vessel.
>
> **Mental** ~ your mental health is the difference between living in pain and living in peace. It controls your psychological well-being because it affects how you feel, think and act. It may also affect your physical well-being.
>
> **Emotional** ~ just like mental health, your emotional stability affects your range of emotions and your behavior. When you understand your emotions and are able to control them, you are better able to handle life's challenges, build strong relationships that can support you through those challenges, and recover from the setbacks that will inevitably come.
>
> **Financial** ~ money makes the world go round and having a dollar in your pocket at all times for some is a blessing.

Accessible finances give us the freedom to live without being dependent on the charity of others. You can not live in freedom, if you are not financially stable.

Family ~ this area for some is most important. Our love for family and their support is the motivation that keeps us alive and grinding, however, we have to also be available to the same family to offer support and provide laughter and love. Additionally, we have to know when to recognize the need to retreat from those closest to us, and to eliminate their opportunities to take advantage, as some often will do.

Love ~ having genuine love in your life is the key to accepting who you are and enjoying the journey you have initiated for yourself. When you love yourself unconditionally, you teach people how to love you as well or you remove the ones who won't. Love is your manual to living an unapologetic life.

Dreams ~ dreams are like flowers, they need to be nurtured, watered, and given lots of love and positive energy. Every day we dream about a vacation, living debt-free, or getting married. For my entrepreneurs, we dream about getting that business up and running, or closing that million-dollar deal. Dreams give us goals to pursue and push us to achieve more.

As you can see, there are many areas that require your attention, all areas that come together and make YOU. If one or more of these areas are dysfunctional or having technical difficulties, your mental and emotional states run the risk of shutting down. We then find ourselves asking for permission, asking for help, or falling into a state of depression, which if in that place for long, can lead to us quitting. Now in some instances, quitting may not be a bad thing because the issue may not be that you did something wrong but that the situation is not your cross to bear.

Knowing when to release, to let go, is just as important as knowing when to hold on. As I referenced in chapter 2, holding on longer than needed is a choice, not a requirement, especially when it comes to learning a lesson. If you touched a hot pot, would you hold on until your skin began to blister in order to feel the temperature fully, or would you let go as soon as the heat burns your skin? That pot and you holding on to something that is detrimental to you is the same thing. Sometimes you need to let go, however, quitting at the first sign of adversity is a no-no. I knew my transformation was going to be difficult, because so many people were used to the "old" me. Telling them "no" only created additional barriers from them in their "old me" mentalities. It was in this adversity that I learned and gained the strength to say NO and be effective in the delivery of it. How can someone force you to remain the same? Anyone who does not want to see you grow should not have the honor of being in your life. I allowed my ""No" to become a complete sentence", with no further explanation necessary, nor given. Nor did I entertain the backlash. Warning: Before you can reach your ultimate goal of transforming your life, you must set goals of growth, for every area of your life, so that ALL of YOU is embedded with positivity.

Setting goals for some are easy, but staying committed to them is more often the chore. That is why setting attainable goals with realistic timeframes is so important! It is heartbreaking to set a goal and start working towards it, and everything just falls apart. Sometimes this happens because we make mistakes in the identification of our goals. At times, we set a goal that was unattainable in the first place, or we did not fully educate ourselves on how to execute the goal. Other times you are trying to accomplish the goals on your own without using the resources available to you, and still more often, your goal is so extreme that it needed to be dismantled and rebuilt by taking smaller steps, and achieving them one by one. Sometimes we allow our goals to get so big that they overwhelm us, and we feel defeated even before we begin. We forget that there are levels that we have to traverse in order to make it to the finish line. For example, I told myself in 2014 that I was going to start a savings account and get out of debt. These goals sound attainable and easy, right? I had a job and a writing career; I wanted to be able to achieve these goals within a year. In order to make that happen, I wasn't able to just start putting money in the bank and paying off credit cards randomly, I needed to check the steps, and hit the levels one by one, so I created a budget and a plan.

Let me show you how I accomplished my goal, step by step, and without disrupting my life, but with a successful finish.

Goal: Fixing my Credit/Removing Debt:

    Step One: I pulled my credit report and got all of my credit cards with balances and the ones with derogatory ratings.

    Step Two: I made a list of all my balances and created a monthly budget paying off the lower balances off first.

WIN

    Step Three: I contacted Lexington Law to assist me in writing letters to the creditors with the derogatory ratings and asked them to remove them from my credit report, especially if the credit was paid.

    Step Four: I implemented my budget and created automatic drafts from my account so that the payment was taken automatically, preventing me from forgetting to make it.

WIN

    Step Five: I followed up with the creditors to speak to them about the status of my removals and further explained the importance of these inquiries being removed as per consumer rights laws.

WIN

Step Six: I checked credit card balances monthly by calling directly, and as one card was paid off, I took the amount of that payment and added it to the amount of the card with the next highest balance, sometimes doubling my payments.

Step Seven: I created a Credit Karma account to watch my debt clear and my score rise.

Step Eight: I moved myself into a position to be able to enjoy financial freedom!

#WINNING!!!!!

Surprisingly, I cleared all of my credit cards in 6 months, and had my credit score, which started at 520, to above 700, in only 13 months. As you see, I set a goal, established a plan, and walked myself through the plan step-by-step, until I had reached the goal! With the attainment of each milestone of paying off the credit cards, I celebrated by cutting up each card as it reached a balance of $0.00. For all of my financially astute people, I did not close the account, I just cut up the cards so that I wouldn't fall back into old habits! The worst thing you can do is get out of debt only to get back in because you have an "available balance". Now don't think that I woke up one morning with the knowledge and understanding of how to become debt free and a fan of financial freedom, I had help from a family member.

Let's Have an Open and Honest Conversation:

After my divorce, I lived in a nice, comfortable two-bedroom apartment with my 2 sons. It was not where I wanted us to be, but it was the beginning of our regrouping and the start of a new life for us all. As my boys got older, I knew it was time for us to spread out, especially since my baby boy was still sleeping with me, so looking for a house became the master plan. At this time, my credit score was as low as it could go, and my savings account was empty, so moving was out of the question. However, one day, I was scrolling through my Facebook feed, and God answered my prayers. I saw that my brother had posted the availability of a three-bedroom house that he was renting in Upper Darby, Pennsylvania. Even though it was across the city and away from the kids' schools, and some distance from my job, it was the space and place that we needed. And, he was only going to charge me $750.00 per month to stay there. Can you say #WINNING!!! I didn't hesitate! I took the place and moved in on November 30, 2014, it was a cute house, and the kids loved it. Craig now had his own room, Chris had a bigger room, and finally, we had a porch again, and kids in the neighborhood to play with. It felt like we were living in an episode of "The Jeffersons". Just like anything else, cheap or free normally comes with a price that often exceeds what you expected. In March, my brother began telling me that the neighborhood was getting bad and that he was looking for me another house in a different neighborhood. On June 3, 2015, I receives a call, from my father, informing me that I would have only 27 days to move out. Now, let me remind you, I had just moved there on November 30' 2014, and then built Rome in a day by buying and decorating the kids' new rooms. Therefore, there was no savings, my credit was still bad because I had not paid any of my bills as my intent was using all that I had to make our house a home. And now, we were faced with having to move again. This situation brought to mind the moment when I stood in Landlord/Tenant court, in front of a judge and an attorney, who told me that if my rent was not paid in full by December 30, 2008, I would have to vacate my apartment. You got it! I was sued in court for non-payment of rent, and had a judgment placed against me. Even though it was my ex-husband who failed to pay the rent for three months, I was held responsible because the lease was in my name. I had to pay it. Talk about marital debt and divorce drama!! By the grace of God, and with the help of a great friend, I was able to avoid being evicted. In this situation with my brother, however, I had no other option but to move out. I had 27 days to move from our house that we had grown to love, with nowhere to go. At that time, I felt so helpless, lost, and confused, not able to understand how I could be in this same situation again. I was beginning to panic! Amazingly, God stepped in yet again, and I was informed that my aunt was moving from her home in Roslyn. My mother interceded and asked her if I could stay there and with no thought, my aunt said, YES!! So on June 27, 2014, two days from my birthday, we moved into our new home. From this experience, I learned so many important lessons. The first lesson, I should have never moved to Upper Darby in my financially unprepared state, and have no back-up plan. Secondly, this experience taught me how family can hurt you even more so than strangers, and quite often, the ones you expect to help you, are the ones who leave you hanging out to dry. After I was advised that I had to move, the only people who assisted me were my mom, my man at the time, and two friends. I depleted my bank account, and I was not able to pay my bills (so that I could pay for the U-haul truck and other moving expenses). Talk about a long 2 weeks between one paycheck and the next!! Third, I learned that good credit and a savings account is imperative to being successfully prepared for the unexpected things that occur in life. If I had a savings account or good credit, things would have happened so very differently. Instead of crying, I would have been able to sign a new lease the next day. This experience, as you can see, made me look at my finances and credit in the harshest way and realize just how unprepared I was. It motivated me to fix the lifeline to my future. I could not go anywhere in other areas of my life if my finances were not in order. In spite of the hurt and anguish that I experienced through this ordeal, it taught me the power of being prepared. Think about your life, and how things in your life might change in the blink of an eye. If your house or apartment was destroyed due to fire, flood, or any other act of nature, do you have an emergency fund or good credit that can guarantee you a place to stay within a couple of hours? Do you have renter's insurance that can help pay for any damages or replace your belongings? Are you prepared for the worst? I was not, and I paid a significant cost, not just once, but twice, and you can best believe, there won't be a third time. Finances are the heartbeat to living prepared, and as my testimony has proved, if it's not functioning at its highest potential, you are 2 steps away from a disaster. I can't express how grateful I was for my mom and aunt (God rest her soul), and the efforts that they put forth to help us. They RESCUED us! Unfortunately, many of us have few people in our lives on whom we can depend for that kind of relief. Most of us have no one. To prevent this situation from happening again, I became focused on cleaning up my credit. I set a goal, planned it out, and got to work. I joined Lexington Law, and they started me on my journey to credit repair. I got busy educating myself about my finances, and learned how to better manage my income, and, most importantly, I learned how to SAVE. The lessons I took away from financial expert and news anchor Nicole Lapin, I continue to use even today. She made understanding my finances easier, and I hit the ground running. She gave me a formula that I still use in my day-to-day monitoring of my finances. In her book, *"Rich Bitch"*, she suggested organizing your money in the following manner:

* **Essentials:** housing, food, insurance and travel. These bills should add up to **70%** of total income.
* **End game:** savings, investments and retirement plans. These bills should be no less than **15%** of total income, and, if at all possible, should be more.
* **Extras:** Fun money, entertainment, going out and splurges. These should be no more than **15%**. "Take out cash, hard green cash, each month," she says. "Once the cash is gone, the party is over."

In order to maintain my financial freedom and increase my savings account, I divided my paychecks up into these percentages, and watched my stress over financial concerns fade away. I made my money work for me and removed from my life this concept of finances as a "hardship". When we educate and become aware of what's holding us back, we then have to make the conscious decision to either eliminate the problem, or find someone who is capable of helping us where we may not be able to help ourselves. There is NO SHAME in asking for help! There is only shame in remaining in a negative or unhealthy situation longer than needed because of your own refusal to seek assistance. The only way you can get to the point of attaining and celebrating your goals is by knowing that you are capable and then setting a plan that will get you where you need to go. It will not be easy, nor will it be without its barriers and challenges, and it will require you to be honest, authentic, and committed, to yourself and your dreams. Now that I have shared my goals, and how I attained the rewards of reaching those goals, think about some of the goals you might want to set for yourself. Think about the individual steps you will need to accomplish in order to fulfill these goals. Pick two goals that are important to you, that you may have been putting off, or have never even attempted to consider before today. Identify every step that needs to be completed (and what resources you might need to complete the steps), and list them below. This will help you to visually SEE your plan, and show you what needs to be done. Create a timeline for yourself, so that you have specified times that you want to have the individual steps completed, and include those dates below as well. Please feel free to add additional steps if needed! Now, prepare yourself for the WIN!! There's nothing like looking at your goal, and embracing it as Mission Accomplished!!

Goal # 1

_____

Target Date: _____

    Step one:

    _____

    _____

Step Two:
_____
_____

Step Three:
_____
_____

Step Four:
_____
_____

Step Five:
_____
_____

Goal #2
_____ Target Date: _____

Step one:
_____
_____

Step Two:
_____
_____

Step Three:

Step Four:

Step Five:

Additional Goals and Target Dates (to be addressed at a later date if need be):

_____
_____TD:_____

_____
_____TD:_____

_____
_____TD:_____

_____
_____TD:_____

TO KEEP IT OR RETURN IT!!

How are you feeling now? I have given you a lot of information, encouraged you to own your life story, and hopefully helped you to understand the importance of acknowledging, accepting and attaining your life's goals. Please recognize, right here, and right now, that you will never make it on the other side of success if you first don't do the work required to help you climb over. Now, here comes the hard part! Brace yourself, because this section to follow is ultimately the part that will separate those who are comfortable in Mediocrity from those who are excited about moving fully into the opportunity of Living.

As Lisa Nichols would say, "I did not come here to entertain you, I came here to make it mildly, to moderately, to significantly uncomfortable for you to live in any form of mediocrity. Mediocrity is crowded, but there is a whole lot of room up in excellence." This book is geared towards challenging you to be excellent, to be greater than average, and better than phenomenal!! This chapter is necessary and vital to you being able to maintain everything you worked so hard for. I don't know anyone who would want to go through what you've gone through to reach this point, have a taste of happiness and liberation, and then want to go back to heartbreak and bondage. I used to hear people say, "you can't free a slave who doesn't know they are in enslaved", so I have to ask you, do you even know that your need of validation, permission, and approval is keeping you imprisoned to those whom you have given permission? This bondage is slavery as well, just without the chains of course! Asking for anything that pertains to your own growth is a form of dependency that keeps you from living at your highest potential. I am here to assist you to break the chains and help you obtain the key that will unlock your padlock so you can walk in your purpose. I want you to be able to absorb this information so it can permeate and reach all the way to your soul. I want it to bubble within your spirit, making you fully committed to applying these principles to your life every day, and every minute of every day. You owe it to yourself to be happy! You owe it to yourself to be successful! You owe it to yourself to know what abundant living is! Think about that place you always dreamed of traveling to, you owe it to yourself to go there! Now think about why you haven't planned your vacation yet. It is time for you to say to yourself, "I deserve my life and I am going to live it according to my own definition." I am here to speak to your mind and help you say, "I can do it!" The only thing that is keeping you from your destiny is YOU! As you can see, I am just now learning that! Better late than never, and now that I know better, I do better. As Lisa Nichols would say, "I am not a fast learner, I am a thorough learner". So yes, while it may have taken me 15 years to reach my definition of living, I put in the work, and paid the price, and learned the lessons needed that has now inspired me and motivated me to remain in my authentic lane! No amount of foolishness could make me go back to where I came from, living paycheck to paycheck, being mentally and emotionally broken, and teaching my children that struggle is the norm for living. Lies! Lies! Lies! There is no pain that we should seek to bring upon ourselves purposefully. So, if you were not born to pain, why are you so determined to live in it! I am here to tell you that it is never too late to change your mindset, remove the pain, and put yourself first. Some people can transform their lives in 2 years and for others it may take 67 years, but it is not how long it takes for you to recognize the need of change, but that you take the action needed to make that change. Allow me to warn you however, you should always try to appreciate the full extent of the storm while you are in the midst of it. Meaning, sometimes you have to weather the storm through to its completions in order to fully understand the lesson, and feel the pain associated, so that you embrace the sun when it returns. My storm lasted 15 years, not allowing me the green light to enjoy life until the lessons learned were ingrained completely. Now that you know what you need to do to give notice, and you are ready to tell people your agenda, rather than being coerced into theirs, we need to explore how you go about maintaining your new freedom. Many will tell you, obtaining something is easy, but maintaining it can be the struggle. I disagree, for many reasons. I believe that it should be easy to maintain things that we truly desire and value. We may face setbacks along the way, but if we have it, and truly appreciate it, and believe in its value to us, we have the capacity to easily retain it. I have never witnessed anyone who threw away something they valued. Think about it this way, if you want something badly enough you will find a way to receive it and hold on to it. If you have found yourself having lost something that you originally worked to obtain, then you at some point, must question if it was really something that you truly wanted in the first place. In your new reality, and within the new space of honesty and authentic ownership of your life, YOU decide if letting go is in your best interest. And if it is not, then YOU decide to do the work to maintain the situation at hand.

Sometimes people, situations, and things require a revision as to their status and place in your life. Their purpose may need to be re-evaluated, and their usefulness applied differently at the new levels that you have attained thus far. Understanding that concept will allow you more latitude as it pertains to maintaining yourself in the levels that you achieve along this journey towards freedom and authentic happiness.

So let's discuss how you can work to maintain all of the progress that you have now made in your lives. How do you hold onto the blessings and favor that you have worked so hard to obtain? Listed below are some of the concepts that I use, even now, to maintain and continue to progress along my journey, as I strive to fulfill and enhance my newly purposed destiny.

Declare ownership of your life: No one can take anything away from you that you don't give away. Your new life is for you to enjoy and enhance as you see fit. Remember you don't need permission to birth and rebirth purposeful milestones and attainable wins. All you need to know and keep in the forefront of your mind is that your happiness and peace is yours to control in its entirety.

Accept your journey, no matter what: There will always be naysayers and shade throwers that will try to throw you off course, but this is where perseverance and determination comes in. You can not be moved if you are deeply rooted in your authenticity. Accept your decisions and move according to your own direction. Learn from the consequences and reap the rewards. Ask for help if you require assistance, but even in that, take away the meat and throw away the bone.

Love and celebrate yourself daily: Every day you will learn something new about yourself. Some days, you will endure hardships that might alter your life story, others you may gain victories that will elevate your story. Either way, celebrate both! Love yourself enough to know that the lesson is worth the time to investigate, and is worth the energy to apply for better results. Everything that happens to us is meant to educate us, not hinder us, so use it to move forward instead of falling backwards.

Affirm that you deserve it: Having this new sense of fulfillment in my life, I often find myself questioning or asking, "What did I do to deserve this?" or "Why me?". I questioned myself so frequently, until finally, I heard the answer, "Why not you?". It was in that moment that I understood, and then I stood solidly on the fact that I am just as deserving of happiness as the next person.

Don't sweat the small stuff: Everyone knows that when good things happen, bad things find a way to insinuate themselves to lessen the impact of that which is good. Know that there will always be obstacles and trials that will occur, but when we plan ahead for the "what ifs" and/or emergency situations, we can approach them with less fear, and move through them with more confidence. Living a liberated life is about being proactive within life. Planning ahead for the unexpected will keep you from having to regress, or return to situations you previously removed yourselves from.

Change your circle: You cannot be friends with, and continue to associate with people who want to keep you living in your past. You cannot embrace the new you if you are constantly being reminded of the old you. Eventually, the new you will have to leave behind the old friends, and gain a circle of like-minded people whose energy, desire, and commitment to accountability rises to a level that matches your own.

Get an accountability partner: I absolutely love my accountability partners. I have two accountability partners, my children, who count as 1, and my man. I chose them because they know what I want to do, and know what I need to do to achieve it. They keep me focused and motivated to get the job done, even when I want to slack off, or be lazy, or even just chill. My business coach is another accountability partner. She will ask me in a minute, "What's new with you?", and if I say nothing, then comes the 50 questions and the ensuing motivation. Your partner should be that extra boost of determination that comes when you need it most, that will push you forward to your goals.

De-clutter your life: The easiest way to begin to rebuild your life with positivity and happiness is to start by letting go of everything, and everybody that goes against the grain of what you are trying to accomplish. Never allow anyone to insult your intelligence by talking you into staying when you know your time is up in that situation. When you are walking towards your freedom and purpose, you will have to be willing to terminate whoever it may be; friends, relationships, partners, and even family members. You cannot bring baggage into your peace. Be ready, and let go and let God.

Be Honest about your Truth. You will never be able to fully elevate your life if you are not completely honest about your desires and intentions. You will never receive your full blessings if you are not open to what your heart is saying. Your truth gives you the ability to be loved and accepted in a manner that is respectful of who you are striving to become. When you speak the truth about yourself, you leave no room for misinterpretation or misunderstanding. Never give anyone reason to make assumptions about your meaning, be open enough to say what you mean and allow them the opportunity to either accept what you are saying, and be there for your journey, or exit, stage left. Not being honest with those around you, or withholding your entire truth, is not only lying to others, but also to yourself. If no one else deserves the unapologetic version of you, YOU DO!

Now I am sure there a many additional ways that we could come up with, that would help you be able to maintain your happiness and liberation, but the ones listed above are those with which I identified the most, and that worked best FOR ME. Take from them what you will, use from them what you can, add to them what you feel is needed, and continue to WORK YOUR PLAN! My accountability partners still push me to surpass my "now" by planting seeds to generate a higher level in my "next". You should never allow yourself to get comfortable in the new life you are building right now. That life is only for the "now", because as you build, your desire to improve upon even what you have already made better should be pushing you forward to your next. Your ability to conquer is limited only by the way that you view the challenges set before you. Never limit yourself to what you have in front of you. Always aim for more, and make sure that whatever it is that you aim to attain, that it will continue to add value and substance to your journey.

And now, after being coached, educated, motivated, and inspired to **STOP** asking for permission and give notice, will you move forward into what could be a place of peace and freedom, or will you remain just where you were before you read this book? As you think about that, answer the following questions to help you determine which direction you might want to go:

If I were given the opportunity to change my life, I would change:

_____
_____
_____
_____
_____
_____
_____

Remaining in my "old" mindset, means that I would continue to accept:

_____
_____
_____
_____
_____
_____
_____

If I am to be able to live the life I desire, I will need to change the following things that bring negativity to my life:

_____
_____
_____
_____
_____

To be effective in my life I would need to do the following things:

To be more effective in my relationships I would need to do the following things:

In order to gain my happiness in LIFE, I will need to be willing to lose:

Their perception of you is none of your business, but your perception of your life will dictate how you will live it.

WHAT IS YOUR INTENTION?

I pray that by the time you have reached this chapter, you have made the conscious decision to take back the power that you abdicated to others, and step into your authentic lane. I pray that I have given you some fundamental gems that you will be able to use to build the foundation, which will lead to the new and improved you. As you were reading this book, I hope you noticed that I did not ask of you anything that I did not first ask of myself. I have always found that lessons are best explained to others by those who have lived through and learned from them. Each lesson that I have shared with you, I have already tested in my personal life. I have learned so much from so many who have shared their personal experiences and the lessons that they learned from those experiences. There is something so moving about hearing a message in the personal testimony of the lessons a person is learning. I am hoping that my lessons learned helped just one person do the same: Learn lessons and share them with someone else who needs to grow. This is what motivates me to share my story.

My ability to be transparent hopefully allows me to be a motivation and inspiration to others, as well as myself. I use my story and my successes as a means to coach someone else to theirs. I am that vessel that will happily tell you what I did, and how I did it, and encourage you to believe that you can do it too. There is nothing in my life that you can't yourself obtain.
From my dreams to my freedom, you have the ability to accomplish similar things, and the first step is to own your life. When I stopped living my life for others and realized my own purpose, I started upon this journey to living without apology. I still say "I'm sorry" if I hurt someone's feelings, but I am no longer sorry for who I was, or who I was trying to become. I am no

longer ashamed of what I want, or how I received what I wanted. I set my own standards and played by my own rules in order to live according to my OWN purpose. I can now admit that after 15 years of living a lie, I built the strongest and boldest platform upon which to build my future. My new strength is resilient and fearless. All of the hell and turmoil that I was able to overcome, has brought me to this place today, and I desire the same for you. As I have said in almost every chapter, YOU DESERVE IT! Do you want better? Then go get it! I often tell people, "The fastest way to get to your dream is by living like you are already in it". It is my hope that you will be able to use this book as a tool to prepare you for your ultimate breakthrough. I want you to join me on the other side of the rainbow, but I need you to cleanse your life and eliminate your baggage, in order for you to get there. It's time for you to clean house and fix your life, so you can honestly and truthfully be a part of the successes. Again, I am not telling you anything I have not already done. I did the work, I read the books, I organized my life, I created the budget, and I gave everything a place, leaving me with nothing more to do but enjoy the fruits of it all. Working paycheck to paycheck is sustainable, but working and not paying attention to payday is much less stressful, and so much more rewarding. How would you like it if you were able to fire your boss and became the C.E.O of your own time and dreams? How awesome would it be if you could leave your unsupportive mate/partner/spouse and find a person who not only wants to support you but vows also to invest in YOU? All of this is possible if you believe that you are worthy of it. Any of this is possible if you will eliminate those things or people, which hinder you from completing your goals. Saying goodbye to the norm may be difficult, but saying hello to the extraordinary is beyond breathtaking. When you own your life, you own your legacy, and that, my friend, is what others will remember you by. If you do not wish to be remembered as the person that you are, in the place in which you are, right now, then allow that to be the motivation to get started on your transformation, if you haven't already started with the previous chapters.

What is your intention in your life? What is your specific purpose for living your life? Are you living in it right now? If not, then list below what you will permanently change from this day forward to change your perception about owning your life:

1. _____
   _____
   _____

2. _____
   _____
   _____

3. _____
   _____
   _____

4. _____
   _____
   _____

I hope you made the things on this list attainable and realistic. Remember, when setting goals, you must be truthful about your limitations, honest about the things you are and are not willing to do, and committed to see these things through to the end. Your journey is not anyone else's. It is solely yours, and must be traversed in a way that will allow you to accept what is beyond your control. Your journey should be outlined according to what you are sure you are able to endure. We all have our own way of achieving success and moving forward to our happiness, and my only goal is that you will find that pot of gold at the end of your rainbow. I am in the business of inspiring individuals to be the greatest champions they can be while living on this thing called earth. The icon entertainer Prince said it best with his lyrics, "Dearly beloved, we are gathered here today, to get through this thing called "life"; and that's all any of us is trying to do, get through this thing called life. So, let's run this race, and let's go crazy together at the finish line! What influences one, will affect another, so we will allow our successes, and even our failures, to elevate our lives overall. Remember, people make the world go round and I want to ensure that we are all being touched with positive karma daily.

So to circle back to the topic at hand, what is your intention now that you have another perspective on living an abundant and authentic life? What will you do with the information given? Will you use my real life examples and apply the lessons to better your life? Will you take living seriously and get started pursuing your dreams?

What will you do now, now that you know better?

WELCOME TO THE "NEW" LIFE

Welcome to the world of the new you. If you honestly did the work, nothing in this world will look familiar to you. Let me be the first to say, congratulations for making it this far and being committed to moving your life forward. There will be a lot of happiness, success and prosperity waiting for you. I may have ruffled a few feathers in previous chapters, but know that the tough talk was done out of my sincere dedication to seeing you own what is rightfully yours. As you now know, I lived the story and paid the price for becoming a visitor in my own life. It feels great to participate in my future and set a course that is rewarding for me. Are you ready to do the things that you've never done? It is time to replace everything from the old you with the new you, so this chapter will help you integrate some new actions and words into your daily life.

When we think about changing our life and mindset, we have to change the way we communicate, and the way that we interact with others. I am a big fan of affirmations and even though I listed the affirmations I spoke into my existence daily, I would like to offer you 20 more of my most favorite quotes that will not only toughen your mindset, but will hopefully increase your motivation to change your life.

1. Make each day your masterpiece. --*John Wooden*
2. Your imagination is your preview of life's coming attractions. --*Albert Einstein*
3. Someday is not a day of the week. --*Denise Brennan-Nelson*
4. It's time to start living the life you've imagined --*Henry James*
5. Always stay grateful, best revenge is your paper. --*Beyoncé*
6. The difference between ordinary and extraordinary is that little extra. --*Jimmy Johnson*

7. All our dreams can come true--if we have the courage to pursue them. --*Walt Disney*
8. Always be a first-rate version of yourself, instead of a second-rate version of somebody else. --*Judy Garland*
9. If you cannot do great things, do small things in a great way. --*Napoleon Hill*
10. It is never too late to be what you might have been. --*George Eliot*
11. Your time is limited, so don't waste it living someone else's life. --*Steve Jobs*
12. The only way to do great work is to love what you do. --*Steve Jobs*
13. Life is what happens to you while you're busy making other plans. --*John Lennon*
14. Don't worry about failures; worry about the chances you miss when you don't even try. --*Jack Canfield*
15. Tough times never last, but tough people do. --*Robert Schuller*
16. Dream big and dare to fail. --*Norman Vaughan*
17. You may be disappointed if you fail, but you are doomed if you don't try. --*Beverly Sills*
18. Too many of us are not living our dreams because we are living our fears. --*Les Brown*
19. Limitations live only in our minds. But if we use our imaginations, our possibilities become limitless. --*Jamie Paolinetti*
2o. It does not matter how slowly you go, as long as you do not stop. --*Confucius*

As you can see, quotes/affirmations are very important to me. I believe that speaking life into your spirit will awaken your desire to explore that life. What we tell ourselves can be vital to whether we move forward or remain stuck in an unhappy present. Positive self-talk is essential for positive outcomes. In addition to positive affirmations, we need to also consider how we communicate, both with ourselves, and with others. When you talk about your past, do you speak as the victim or the victor? Do you blame the person who did you wrong or do you own your role in the matter and use the behaviors as a learning lesson? When we change the way we address our story, we take back the power of our past in such a way that it leaves no room to interrupt our future. For example, you may have noticed that I often say, "I allowed" or "I gave", which implies that I have acknowledged my role in the situation and the authority that I have in these situations. I can't be upset when people treat me with disrespect, but I can instead accept my own culpability for allowing them the opportunity to treat me that way. People and life will only do to you what you allow, and allowing anything that is not in accordance to your newness is detrimental to your growth. So today, I challenge you to speak in your truth. Own your actions and love the lessons connected. When you accept your life, you will begin to love and protect everything in it especially yourself. Love is another attribute to maintaining the newness in your life, thus making it that much harder for you to let it go.

Now that you have read this book, what have you learned about yourself and your journey? Are you ready to stop asking for permission about your life? Are you ready to tell some people where they can go with their opinions? Lastly, as you ready to simply live? If you said yes, then I challenge you to implement what you learned, explore your truths when answering the coaching questions that were given, learn from my mistakes, and always remember that your authenticity will define your accountability. If you are honest about who you are, you will keep true what you say you want and be eager to begin the process. Before you get to work implementing and rebirthing, understand your ability to take as many chances, you need to get it right. As you consider these things, I want you to write a letter to the new you. Speak to yourself with a voice of encouragement and manifest what you want. Let the new you know what you expect and what you will not tolerate. Be clear! Be honest! Most importantly, be unapologetic about what you now want. You are the person with the power to make things happen.

You can't grow with toxic waste surrounding you. I want you to be so open and honest in this letter, that after you write it, it becomes your manual of what to do next. "What comes next" is a big thing for me, and reviewing the tools, tips, and thoughts as we discussed them, provides much of what you need to get you started on your track. If you can't be honest with yourself about who you are and what you want, then who can you be vulnerable with? It's time to peel back the outer layers, and get to work, from within!

Dear Old Me,

_____
_____
_____
_____
_____
_____
_____
_____
_____
_____
_____
_____
_____
_____
_____
_____
_____
_____
_____
_____
_____
_____
_____
_____

Sincerely,
The New Me

PART 2:
30 DAYS OF SELF-TRANSFORMATION

Now you all know that I could not stop there! I could not leave you guessing, assuming or trying to figure out how to get started on your journey to new living. When I said I wanted to see you on the other side of the rainbow, I meant it. I know I gave you a lot of information and I hope that I also provoked a lot of thought. Now all I need is to assist you in being able to implement and apply action to all I have said. Many of the steps that you have read about, I have lived through. A true coach will not only coach you towards your goals and dreams, they will give you instructions and detailed action steps that are meant to spur you to get up off of the couch, and project you into the life you want.

The next part of this book, 30 days to Self-Transformation, will include exercises which will hopefully challenge you to move from being average to becoming extraordinary. You will explore what it means to change your lifestyle, and begin the difficult task of starting a savings account. You will receive suggestions to implement to make changes in your life, and accept your responsibility for that life. "30 Days" is not just a section that you read to finish out the book. It's the section that will push YOU to work towards your successes. This book will only work if YOU work it, so I challenge you today to do the hard work needed to get you moving towards giving your notices. Some things in this section may not apply to you, some of you may already be doing some of the activities listed, but I am sure there is something in your life that need to be changed, adjusted, or removed, or that is not adding value to your life. On this day, as you read this section, I am challenging you to step outside of your comfort zone and get familiar with the unknown. That unknown has the potential to lead you to your purpose. As some people will tell you, success sits on the other side of failure. YES!!! Your success in your ability to give notice will only blossom if you are able to give those notices with the conviction borne of faith.

It's time for you to jump in with your eyes closed and your mind open, ready to receive all that you are due along the way. When you allow yourself the opportunity to explore life rather than just simply living it, you get the most out of the time you lived. "This world doesn't owe me anything", is a saying my aunt Margaret Tolliver, used to say frequently. She did not have unrealistic expectations as to what would be coming her way from "the world". She understood firsthand that whatever she wanted, she needed to work for, and whatever she set out to achieve, she needed to WORK for. She walked through pain, shook hands with heartbreak, adjusted her crown as she waded through mediocrity, and she stood tall throughout her life, in order to own her happiness. When she passed, there was not in dry eye at her funeral but there was a calm in the atmosphere because everyone there celebrating her was well aware that she lived her life in both an unapologetic and fully authentic way. Having her as my mentor and aunt, gave me a shining example of the things that could be done.

So if you are ready, let's start this 30 day transformation and begin the process of applying new ideas, new thoughts, new activities, and new successes to our world. This world is too big for you to live in a box….

Day 1 of our 30 Day Self Transformation

Physical Makeover. It's time to go through your wardrobe, carefully look at your appearance, and pay attention to your emotions. Your appearance plays a big part of how you feel about yourself on a day to day basis, or see yourself inside and out. So today, go get your hair done, manicure, pedicure, go shopping for something with a splash of color to brighten your outfits... I want you to look in the mirror and not recognize something about you. The person you saw waking up this morning should not be the same person you smile at going to sleep this evening.

What did you do to implement this exercise?

_____
_____
_____
_____
_____
_____
_____

The hardest part of this exercise was...

_____
_____
_____
_____
_____
_____
_____

Day 2 of our 30 Day Self Transformation

Rebirth yourself with love, confidence, enjoyment, happy thoughts and positive images... Speak life back into yourself. Manifest the thoughts you know will keep your attitude positive. Let no one get under your skin. Control your feelings and think only of things that will enhance your day. You become what you think, so today it's all about engraving a new mentality!! Think it, say it, live it!!!!

What did you do to implement this exercise?

_____
_____
_____
_____
_____
_____
_____
_____

The hardest part of this exercise was…..

_____
_____
_____
_____
_____
_____
_____
_____

Day 3 of our 30 Day Self Transformation

Step outside of your "box"!!! We all have this area in our lives where we only do what's comfortable, but living starts when you are most uncomfortable. When you're familiar, you exist...but when you're unfamiliar, you explore, you learn, you go above and beyond to reach your destination. Today do something outside of the norm, something that you've never done, tried, or wore. It may seem strange at first, but after enjoying the experiences, I assure you, it will be worth it.

What did you do to implement this exercise?

The hardest part of this exercise was……

Day 4 of our 30 Day Self Transformation

It's okay to be selfish with your life. Stop giving people an all-access pass to your life. Stop telling social media, your co-workers, and anyone who will listen, the details of your personal business. It's one thing to share your testimony to inspire someone else, it's another thing to be gossiping and boasting for the sake of hearing yourself talk. Everything ain't for everybody, and unless they are willing to invest (and assist), they should have no say. Move in silence, it's harder for people to throw up road blocks if they do not know what you are doing and when you are doing it.

What did you do to implement this exercise?

_____
_____
_____
_____
_____
_____

The hardest part of this exercise was......

_____
_____
_____
_____
_____
_____

Day 5 of our 30 Day Self Transformation

Fitness is maintaining a Healthy Life! Physical Activity and Proper Nutrition are two of the most important ingredients to a healthier lifestyle. Regular exercise will maintain the performance of your lungs and heart to most efficiently burn off excess calories and keep your weight under control. Another benefit of physical activity is that it decreases the risk of heart disease, stroke, colon cancer, diabetes and high blood pressure. Now, good nutrition is just as important because it can also help you to reach and maintain a healthy weight, reduce your risk of chronic diseases, and promote your overall health. So today, I would like you to plan and execute the following: obtain a gym membership, join a Zumba class, and meet with a nutritionist or research healthier food choices. With fitness and proper foods, your energy, stamina, and health will improve.

What did you do to implement this exercise?

_____
_____
_____
_____
_____
_____
_____
_____

The hardest part of this exercise was……

_____
_____
_____
_____

Day 6 of our 30 Day Self Transformation

Health is Wealth, so today we are making appointments to see your Doctors: Primary Care Physicians, Vision, and Dental doctors. Healthcare is so important, and maintaining your health requires timely follow up with the doctors noted above. This will help with early detection of many viruses, diseases, or life-threatening agents. In order to love yourself, your body must be operating at its best. Make your appointments today so you can live a long, long, long life.

What did you do to implement this exercise?

_____
_____
_____
_____
_____
_____
_____

The hardest part of this exercise was......

_____
_____
_____
_____
_____
_____
_____

Day 7 of our 30 Day Self Transformation

Forgiveness is not for them, but for you! You will never fully be able to move on with living your life if you continue to harbor ill will against those that hurt you, abandoned you, denied you, or have forsaken you a piece of your mind and heart. So today, I want you to face that pain that you are holding by either calling that person, writing them a letter, or speaking it out loud in a silent room, telling them how they hurt you, how it made you feel, and then saying, "But, I forgive you". In addition, I want you to forgive yourself for the damage you may have caused yourself by enduring the pain and holding onto those resentments for so long.

What did you do to implement this exercise?

_____
_____
_____
_____
_____
_____
_____
_____

The hardest part of this exercise was……

_____
_____
_____
_____
_____
_____
_____
_____

Day 8 of our 30 Day Self Transformation

Do something that will excite you today. If you are an employee, mother, wife, husband, member of an organization, father, etc. you know that there is never enough time in a day for YOU. After you tend to everyone else's needs, there is no time remaining for you...at least no awake time. Today, I want you cancel, reschedule, or otherwise adjust your schedule so that YOU can do something for YOU. It can be as simple as sleeping in, going for a walk, having lunch for one, or getting your hair done. No matter what you choose, it must be all about you.

What did you do to implement this exercise?

_____
_____
_____
_____
_____
_____
_____

The hardest part of this exercise was……

_____
_____
_____
_____
_____
_____
_____

Day 9 of our 30 Day Self Transformation

Elevate your life! When you were a young girl or boy, you had a dream of becoming something, living in a particular house, driving a particular car, have a certain amount of money, and working in a big building. Today I want you to think about what your younger self-wanted and what your older self has, or does not have. Did you make your younger person happy? Did you accomplish that dream? If not, today I want you to figure out why or why not, and make a plan to work towards achieving at least 2 of your childhood desires.
What did you do to implement this exercise?

The hardest part of this exercise was……

Day 10 of our 30 Day Self Transformation

Reading is Fundamental! Some people say reading is healing, soothing, allows your mind to wander, gain insight on different topics, and enjoy a great adventure without ever leaving the house. Sometimes a book can take you out of your reality and place you within a story, giving you the excitement and fulfillment of experiencing something greater than your immediate surroundings. In addition to mental stimulation, reading increases your grasp of knowledge, and knowledge is definitely power! It gets no better than that!

What did you do to implement this exercise?

_____
_____
_____
_____
_____
_____
_____
_____

The hardest part of this exercise was…….

_____
_____
_____
_____
_____
_____
_____
_____

Day 11 of our 30 Day Self Transformation

Re-evaluate your circle of friends. Being linked with like-minded people is important to your growth as a person. I have heard people say, "You are the company you keep," so today you must look at the people you associate with, hang with, party with, and otherwise interact with, and make sure that they are beneficial to you in some way. If they are not adding to your life, they are hindering your process. Being a better you requires that you surround yourself with people who understand your vision, see your course and direction, and understand the importance of you getting there. Being successful in your journey will require that the people that you allow closest to you at least support your journey, even if they do not understand or agree with the direction that you have chosen for yourself.

What did you do to implement this exercise?

_____
_____
_____
_____
_____
_____
_____
_____

The hardest part of this exercise was......

_____
_____
_____
_____
_____

Day 12 of our 30 Day Self Transformation

Build your creditworthiness. As you should know, we live in a credit driven society. Everything important that we need to obtain (cars, homes, apartments, college, utilities, cell phones, and so much more) requires credit, and good to excellent credit at that! If you want low interest rates, you need to have a relatively high credit score. Today, I want you to take a step towards building your credit and join Credit Karma. This will allow you to monitor your credit reports and scores. Additionally, I suggest that you request a copy of your credit report (if you haven't done so within the last year) from all three companies, and check them for accuracy. Your credit is your report card for companies when it comes to borrowing or requesting credit and services. If your credit is not where it should be, you definitely should start making strides to fix it.

www.creditkarma.com ~ Instantly receive your free credit score and free credit reports online.

https://www.annualcreditreport.com ~ Get a free copy of your credit report every 12 months from each credit reporting company.

What did you do to implement this exercise?

_____
_____
_____
_____
_____
_____
_____
_____

The hardest part of this exercise was……

_____
_____
_____
_____
_____
_____
_____

Day 13 of our 30 Day Self Transformation

Invest NOW in your retirement. I don't know about you, but I want to retire long before I am 65 so that I can enjoy life. I also know that if I don't plan for it, I will probably be working until the day the good Lord calls me home. Today, we can start planning for the future while we have the time and opportunity. I encourage you to research TODAY the investment/retirement opportunities that are available to you, either through your employer, or through privately funded entities. If you don't already have a 301K or 303B program set up, contact your Human Resources representative and ask about starting one. Meet with a financial planner and see if he/she can come up with a forecast for your future and identify ways to prepare for it, and the goals you need to set to achieve that preparation. When you plan and prepare early, you can rest and enjoy later.

What did you do to implement this exercise?

_____
_____
_____
_____
_____
_____
_____

The hardest part of this exercise was……..

_____
_____
_____
_____

Day 14 of our 30 Day Self Transformation

Family Love is the Best Love! I used to say family are our first friends in life because they teach us how to interact, they gossip, they support us, they can be naysayers, and they are the first group of people with whom we learn day to day interaction. Since we can't pick them, we still have to love them, either in close quarters (for those we get along well with), or from a distance (for those for whom we have less affinity). Today, I would like for you to call, visit, have dinner, or Skype someone in your family. Take the time to laugh, catch up, cry, or to simply say, "I Love you". No matter how crazy, loving, or messy they are, family are the ones that know you the best, and the ones who will be missed and who will miss you when all is said and done.

What did you do to implement this exercise?

_____
_____
_____
_____
_____
_____
_____

The hardest part of this exercise was……

_____
_____
_____
_____
_____
_____

Day 15 of our 30 Day Self Transformation

Apologize to yourself, for hurting yourself! Removing baggage is so vital and important to your growth, and your ability to maintain your progress. As you continue to work on forgiving those that have hurt you, you must also be able to forgive yourself for the self-inflicted pain that you have suffered. People only do to us what we allow, and as much as we want to blame others for our mental and emotional state, we have to look at the role we ourselves played in the hurt that we suffered. So today, I want you to write a letter to your old self, acknowledging and apologizing for everything that you put "YOU" through. After you write the letter to yourself, I want you to read it aloud while standing in front of a mirror, looking at yourself. Once you finish reading, look at yourself and say, "I am SORRY"!

What did you do to implement this exercise?

_____
_____
_____
_____
_____
_____
_____

The hardest part of this exercise was……..

_____
_____
_____
_____
_____
_____

Day 16 of our 30 Day Self Transformation

Improve your prayer life! If you are spiritual, you have heard the saying "prayer changes things". Prayer gives you hope, faith, and strength to proceed in life. When was the last time you considered your prayer life and how it affects your peace of mind? When was the last time you said a prayer? When was the last time that you approached your higher power in prayer for guidance, direction, or to say thank you? Spiritual growth is just as important as physical health. There is power in prayer for those who believe, and there is peace in knowing that your needs will be met by that higher power who is hearing and caring for you. So today, pray for everything, say thank you for everything, and maintain your connection with your higher power.

What did you do to implement this exercise?

_____
_____
_____
_____
_____
_____
_____

The hardest part of this exercise was.......

_____
_____
_____
_____
_____
_____

Day 17 of our 30 Day Self Transformation

Speak life into your existence. I know we covered this area before, but we can never have too much of a good thing, and positive affirmations are always helpful. Today I want you to: Speak to your success. Speak to your love. Speak to your breakthrough. Speak to your transformation. Speak to your healing. Speak to your peace. Speak to your increase. Speak to your clarity. Speak to your confidence. Use your words to infuse your soul. Infuse your body, mind and spirit with positive energy through positive words. Your thoughts become your words, your words become your actions, and your actions become your reality. Start positively so you can arrive at positivity.

What did you do to implement this exercise?

_____
_____
_____
_____
_____
_____
_____

The hardest part of this exercise was……

_____
_____
_____
_____
_____
_____
_____
_____

Day 18 of our 30 Day Self Transformation

Take a Vacation. If you are like many of us, you need a break from the day-to-day issues of life, and a vacation from the everyday hustle and bustle. I don't know your financial status, but I do know that everyone can make a way to take a needed break to regroup and readjust. If you can't plan a 5 star vacation on the beach, you can still plan a staycation, or take a day trip, or work out a half day of work to go home and sleep for a few extra hours. I do it every chance I get. It is just as effective for me to go to New York and stay overnight in a hotel and then come back home. It may sound crazy, but when I get back I am so rejuvenated. Try it…you will thank me later. I want you to make time for a break, and commit to executing at least one type of break within the next month.

What did you do to implement this exercise?

_____
_____
_____
_____
_____
_____
_____

The hardest part of this exercise was……

_____
_____
_____
_____
_____

Day 19 of our 30 Day Self Transformation

Build multiple streams of revenue! We all know that trying to live comfortably requires more money than we have usually have in any of our accounts. Having multiple streams of revenue helps to ensure that you have cash on hand, and is helpful in enabling you to build savings accounts. If you have a business, gift, talent, or skill inside of you, let it out and allow it to work for you. If you like to write, pen a book and sell it. If you like cars, learn how to fix them. If you like to coach people, become a life coach and charge for your services. Instead of throwing away your old clothes, start an online clothing business through pre-created sites. There are multiple ways that you can receive revenue, but you have to find your passion and make it work. As you help others, you are actually earning income to help yourself. Win-Win, right??? Pick an idea, and work to see if you can build that idea into one that will bring you income.

What did you do to implement this exercise?

_____
_____
_____
_____
_____
_____
_____
_____

The hardest part of this exercise was…..

_____
_____
_____

Day 20 of our 30 Day Self Transformation

Attend or join Professional Organizations. Growth in our professional lives can have such a huge impact on our overall life because it gives us (1) a greater feeling of accomplishment, (2) job stability, and (3) a higher level of productivity, which can lead to advancement opportunities. When your professional life is in order, your overall sense of success is heightened. Today search and plan to attend some professional networking events. Research what it will take to join 1 or 2 professional organizations (preferably associated to your current field or business interests) so that you are able to connect and network with others with the same interests and access the resources that others might have knowledge of.

What did you do to implement this exercise?
_____
_____
_____
_____
_____
_____
_____

The hardest part of this exercise was.......
_____
_____
_____
_____
_____
_____

Day 21 of our 30 Day Self Transformation

Tear down those walls. Having walls, boundaries, limitations, and restrictions on your life will only limit your ability to grow into the person you are destined to be. Today, examine the limits and restrictions that you are placing on yourself. Ensure that you are not permitting others in your life to place limitations on you unknowingly. Wherever there is doubt, remove it! Wherever there is fear, remove it! Wherever there are lines drawn in the sand, walk over them! Identify 2 things that might be holding you back or limiting your access. Plan to eliminate those things and set a timeline for you to address and execute the plan. Move forward with that plan within the time frame that you have established.

What did you do to implement this exercise?

_____
_____
_____
_____
_____
_____
_____

The hardest part of this exercise was……

_____
_____
_____
_____
_____
_____

Day 22 of our 30 Day Self Transformation

Plan a romantic evening! Showing love is extremely important in both a relationship, and for yourself. When interacting throughout your life or within the life of another, you must take time out to love on, love with, or do loving things to remind yourself/your partner that they are appreciated, cared for, and needed. For those who are single, you must ensure that you take time out to show the same appreciation for yourself! Treat yourself to something special, buy some flowers, or get a massage. Romancing yourself is just as necessary as maintaining romance between two people. Today, take the time to plan something for this week that will show that you are appreciated, whether with your significant other, or for yourself.

What did you do to implement this exercise?

_____
_____
_____
_____
_____
_____
_____

The hardest part of this exercise was……..

_____
_____
_____
_____
_____
_____

Day 23 of our 30 Day Self Transformation

Estate planning, is in order! Ensure that your affairs are in order BEFORE it is needed. Focus on Life Insurance, Wills, Living Wills, Trust Funds, and Power of Attorney. What will happen should you pass? If you leave this earth today or tomorrow, will your family have the money to pay for your funeral? Will they be able to distribute your assets without fighting? As we focus on living, we must also prepare for death. Losing you is going to be a traumatic moment, but having to raise money, fight with other loved ones, and debating over property can add trauma to an already stressful event. Prepare your family for the inevitable, and give them the gift of your preparation. Today, take the time to research obtaining life insurance (if you don't already have it), review your life insurance policy if you already have one, update your will, or create one, and ensure that your family will know what your wishes are in the event that you are no longer able to verbalize them for yourself. Contact an estate planning attorney and start planning.

What did you do to implement this exercise?

_____
_____
_____
_____
_____
_____
_____
_____

The hardest part of this exercise was.......

_____
_____

Day 24 of our 30 Day Self Transformation

Pray for Increase in your Life! Daily, we are reminded that we can never settle for less when we know we are worthy, deserving, and desire so much more. As my mother would say, "a closed mouth don't get fed" so today, we are going to pray for an increase in our Environment, Finances, Energy, Understanding, Patience, Vision, and Love. The Bible says "ask and it shall be given unto you, seek and ye shall find". And as you pray for increase, pray also for the wisdom to put that increase to good use, and for the ability to be a good steward with the increase that comes. Praying is encouraged.

What did you do to implement this exercise?

_____
_____
_____
_____
_____
_____
_____
_____

The hardest part of this exercise was……

_____
_____
_____
_____
_____
_____
_____

Day 25 of our 30 Day Self Transformation

Step Out On Faith! Today, I want you to consider things that you might want to do, but have always been afraid to do. Think on these things, and prepare yourself to meet a challenge. Choose ONE THING, right now, that you will strive to accomplish. And TRY! So what if you fail! So what if you finish last! Your main focus here is simply to try. It doesn't matter whether or not you actually finish, what matters is that you TRY. Right NOW, identify something, see it through, and be proud of your effort. You can do it!!!

What did you do to implement this exercise?

_____
_____
_____
_____
_____
_____
_____

The hardest part of this exercise was…….

_____
_____
_____
_____
_____
_____
_____

Day 26 of our 30 Day Self Transformation

Volunteer your time! Life can sometimes have us so busy that we forget the importance of community service, volunteering our time to help those in need, inspire others, or make a difference in the lives of others or our communities. "It takes a village to raise a child," is the statement that for so long has held our communities together. Today, that statement still holds true. With the unstable economy, homelessness, identity crises, and mental health issues running rampant through our communities, volunteering your time to help those in need is one of the most rewarding things one can do. There are many organizations that can use your skills, today I challenge you to pick one, and take the time to give back to someone less fortunate than yourself.

What did you do to implement this exercise?

_____
_____
_____
_____
_____
_____
_____
_____

The hardest part of this exercise was…….

_____
_____
_____
_____
_____
_____

Day 27 of our 30 Day Self Transformation

Find ways to CUT your Expenses! Some people live paycheck to paycheck, and some make just enough to survive, still others are barely able to even survive. Today we are going to find ways to cut our expenses. You cannot live only to pay bills and being broke is not beneficial, so it's time to find ways to save money. Look at all of your expenses (utilities and personal) and see if you can downsize or cancel anything. Identify what items are needs, and what are non-essentials. Today, make a point to write out all expenses, down to the smallest item. Pick one item that can be eliminated, and remove that one today. The funds that were used to pay for that item should be redirected into a savings account. It might be a stretch for a bit, but it will feel so good on the long run.

What did you do to implement this exercise?

The hardest part of this exercise was……

Day 28 of our 30 Day Self Transformation

Learn about, and consider investing in stock! Investing in stock may seem risky to some people, but to others it has been a source of great financial gain. Investing is not a "rich man's game" as people often assume it to be. There are many opportunities for those who are interested in learning about investing to start small, and cautiously. There are also opportunities for those who desire to be more aggressive in their investing. Today, I challenge you to at least take a moment to gain some knowledge regarding the tool of investing and how it can be made to work for you. Research what your first steps would be if you were to begin to establish an investment portfolio. You don't have to actually invest if you decide that it is not for you, but you will at least have the information to come back to should you change your mind.

What did you do to implement this exercise?

_____
_____
_____
_____
_____
_____
_____

The hardest part of this exercise was……

_____
_____
_____
_____
_____

Day 29 of our 30 Day Self Transformation

Write a personal mission statement. I want you to think of your journey as a business, as a brand. If you had to sell yourself to someone, what would your 2-minute pitch consist of? Today, I would like you to write your own mission statement. Think about (1.) Why you exist and your reason for being, (2.) What you have to offer and to whom or to what you are devoted to and (3.) How you are committed to maintaining your legacy. After you have given these questions some thought, and sketched some things out, write your statement out and post it where you will always see it! Having a visual of your mission, purpose, and vision, will better help you remain focused on that mission.

What did you do to implement this exercise?

_____
_____
_____
_____
_____
_____
_____

The hardest part of this exercise was.......

_____
_____
_____
_____
_____
_____
_____

Day 30 of our 30 Day Self Transformation

Practice Self-Compassion. Today is all about loving yourself through your words, and removing every negative phrase, word, or comment ever directed towards you, from your mentality. Feeding yourself negativity is never healthy, and just as damaging as if you were physically harming yourself. Instead of criticizing, belittling, or telling yourself how unworthy you are, provide strength, speak life, and be kind to your mental and emotional being. Once you damage how you view yourself, you damage your self-esteem and self-confidence. So today, I encourage you to heal the way that you view yourself, be compassionate towards yourself, and lift your self-esteem with positive talk. I would like you to write out a list of negative feelings that you have harbored over the years, and hurtful words that may have been attributed to you in the past. After completing that task, I want you to tear it up the paper, into the smallest possible pieces, and throw it into the trash. As you remove those negative thoughts, you allow your personal mind space to refill with positivity.

What did you do to implement this exercise?

_____
_____
_____
_____
_____
_____
_____

The hardest part of this exercise was……

_____
_____

Celebrate, this is not the end, but the beginning of living the new you!

You made it!!! Throughout this process, you were challenged to identify, face, remove, apologize, forgive, and organize your life so that it can be more pleasing and less stressful for you and everyone in your circle. Today, I would like you to celebrate your successes as you complete this process, as well as prepare yourself to maintain this lifestyle. What is the purpose of self-improvement if you are not willing to maintain it? Self-improvement does not end once you close the book; it requires practice and continuous nurturing. Therefore, as we say goodbye, I want you to say hello and walk into your new direction using the tools and challenges in this book. If you do the work, your life from this point forward will be Rewarding, Peaceful, Meaningful, and Authentically Yours!

THE END

Thank You

I want to thank you for purchasing this book and I look forward to seeing you on this side of happiness. Come to the side where there is abundance, prosperity, love, and excellence. Your life, love and laughter depend on it!

After you close this book, would you please do me the great favor of logging on to either amazon.com or barnesnnoble.com and leave a (hopefully favorable) review of this book? Your review is used to provide me with much needed and desired feedback on your thoughts, and to provide insight and information to others who may be considering making the investment to purchase this book. So if you were moved in any way, or inspired in the slightest, please feel free to say so in your review. Again, I thank you very much, and I greatly appreciate your support.

With Purpose,
Charron

Acknowledgements

This book marks 26 years of my penning my thoughts, feelings, emotions, and experiences. Never in a million years did I think I would end up here! What a journey!

Chief Activator Lucinda Cross, thank you for sharing your gift to this book. Even though, I still have not met you personally, we have developed a sisterhood beyond measure. Thank you for "Activating" my spirit and being an active participant in my journey.

Mommy!!!! None of this would have happened if you had not first recognized the gift in me and then encouraged me to hone that gift. Every time I found myself in trouble and you told me to write, did you know that you were creating a writer. LOL!!!

My Sister…your support, constructive criticism, pointed questions, and unwavering protection was not always easy to swallow, but it has all worked together to help me become more business savvy, and led me to clarity about who and what I am. It's funny how the younger sister had to play the role of the bigger sister sometimes. LOL!! You did a great job! Lesson learned and very much appreciated!

Dad, where do I start? We have come from my dancing on your feet, to you ensuring that I always know that you are my #1 supporter. Our road has been rocky, but the rocks have fallen into just the right places, just when it mattered the most. Thank you for your love and support and for holding my down as "I dared to be great!"

My Boys, Christopher and Craig…I knew from the day I became a mother that I had to be an not just a mother, but also an example and a leader, with no instruction manual. Even though, we have had our moments, you truly have brought out the best in me. I strive every day to be greater so that you can have the best role model ever.

To my Love, who would have known that 14 years later we would be enjoying and living life together again? If our story did not teach me anything else, it has taught me the power of forgiveness. Thank you and I hope you are ready for this crazy ride…

To my Aunts, Uncles, Cousins, Friends, and extended Family…Thank you for the support and love! Your encouragement of me from a baby until now has come to fruition and is now paying off! Aunt Tracy, ***How You Doin***!

Pen Legacy Family
Vaughn, your passion and compassion when it comes to helping others see their greatest potential is priceless. Thank you for your time, our talks, and your diligence in supporting my liberation. Congratulations on your successes and may the universe continue to support your mission, as will I.
Summer, Soror, I thank you for your kitchen table, the birthplace of Pen Legacy Publishing. I went from publishing myself to publishing 6 amazing new authors in a year. What did you tell yourself that you finally told me? I heart you!!
To my editor, Renise, chiiiiiiild this journey was amazing! For this to be your first project, you are truly a pro. Thank you for "getting it" and helping me to speak with the voice that I always wanted to have heard. Finally, I am heard!
Junnita, you already know…LOL! There would be no Pen Legacy were it not for your keen eye for style and graphics.

Special Thanks
I have to shower special thanks for Michael & Monique Burrell, Nicole Cruz, Sallie Jones, Khristina Yates-Barnes, Syleena Johnson, Dr. Syleecia Thompson & The Visionaries, Jaguar Wright, Monique Grant, My Sorors of Zeta Phi Beta Sorority, Inc.,

Brothers of Phi Beta Sigma Fraternity, Inc, Stars and Masons of Ruth Chapter #66, Lisa Washington, Lizz Goins Turner, Lisa Nichols, Nicole Lapin, Steve Harvey, Bishop T. D. Jakes, and Pastor Jerome F. Coleman of First Baptist Church of Crestmont, thank you for the weekly motivation and guidance. I am because you are!!

About the Author

Charron Monaye is a writer who is not afraid to pen the thoughts, feelings, and truths that many hide out of fear. Her body of work spans over two decades to include: five published books, two produced stage plays, two co-writing books, former contributing writer for CNN IReport, and content writer. In addition to building her own empire, she has helped many entrepreneurs build their businesses and brands through her personal coaching, publishing services and motivational books. Her work has been shared and supported by celebrities such as, Actress Meagan Good, Music Manager/Professor at Berkeley College Dr. Syleecia Thompson, Actor Dennis L.A. White, Actress Tamara Bass, to name a few.

Transparent, respectful, and maternal are just a few adjectives used when describing Charron Monaye. She is a woman who is devoted to assisting others to reach their greatest potential by using what she has learned on her journey to help propel others towards theirs. Creating this legacy wasn't always a bed of roses, but with determination and her therapeutic need to write, she mastered the skill of writing her way out of adversity, confusion, and heartbreak.

She is a mother of 2 sons; Christopher and Craig. She has a B.A. in Political Science, Masters in Public Administration, and a certificate in Paralegal Studies and Life Coaching. She is a member of Zeta Phi Beta Sorority, Epsilon Rho Zeta Chapter, Order of Eastern Star, Ruth Chapter #66 (PHA~ PA), and The Visionaries Entrepreneur Network.
Email: charron.monaye@gmail.com
Learn more about Charron Monaye:
- Website: www.penlegacy.com
- Facebook: @penlegacy
- Instagram: @iamcharronmonaye
- Periscope & Twitter: @PenLegacy

Charron Monaye Coaches

The purpose of Charron Monaye Coaches is to improve self-awareness, create an empowering attitude, unleash latent potential, transform one's mindset, increase earning potential, cultivate one's primary life purpose, and facilitate the achievement of personal causes and aspirations that will leave behind a personal legacy. You have started your journey to success, but do you have a map and the resources necessary to arrive at your desired destination?

MY APPROACH TO PERSONAL DEVELOPMENT COACHING IS DESIGNED TO MOTIVATE INDIVIDUAL CLIENTS TO:

- Define one's purpose
- Create an "I CAN" belief system
- Manage emotions, mindset, attitudes, and behaviors
- Live in autonomy (freedom from others' opinions and beliefs)
- Be capable of sustaining healthy interpersonal relationships
- Understanding and maintaining financial freedom
- Live with personal integrity
- Position their entrepreneur skills or dreams

Charron Monaye Coaches is an effective, affordable and convenient way to get you the information you need to build the life of your dreams. In short, we'll show you how we did it! You can sign up for a 30 & 60 minutes sessions or 3 hour monthly coaching sessions that will be geared to your growth, your dreams, and your life. This is an intense and extremely results-driven process that requires you to be open, willing, and available to receiving what is rightfully yours. To learn more visit: http://www.penlegacy.com/charron-monaye-coaches

Additional Books by Charron Monaye

www.ingramcontent.com/pod-product-compliance
Lightning Source LLC
Chambersburg PA
CBHW070621300426
44113CB00010B/1608